Social Environmental Research in the European Union

Social Environmental Research in the European Union

Research Networks and New Agendas

Michael Redclift

Professor of Human Geography and the Environment, Department of Geography, King's College, London, UK

Elizabeth Shove

Director of the Centre for Science Studies, University of Lancaster, UK

Barend van der Meulen

Senior Researcher, Centre for Studies of Science, Technology and Society, University of Twente, The Netherlands

Sujatha Raman

Researcher, Centre for Science Studies, University of Lancaster, UK

With the assistance of:
Alfredo Cadenas, Pablo del Rio,
Liana Giorgi, Heide Hackmann
Pirkko Kasanen

Edward Elgar

Cheltenham, UK • Northampton, MA, USA

Published by
Edward Elgar Publishing Limited
Glensanda House
Montpellier Parade
Cheltenham
Glos GL50 1UA
UK

Edward Elgar Publishing, Inc.
136 West Street
Suite 202
Northampton
Massachusetts 01060
USA

A catalogue record for this book is available from the British Library

Library of Congress Cataloguing in Publication Data
Social environmental research in the European Union : research networks and new agendas / by Michael Redclift . . . [et al.].
   Includes bibliographical references and index.
   ISBN 1-84064-211-4
      1. Environmental policy—Social aspects—Europe. 2. Environmental policy—Economic aspects—Europe. 3. Environmental policy—Research—Europe. 4. Europe—Social policy. 5. Europe—Economic policy. I. Redclift, M. R.

GE190.E85 S63 2000
363.7'0094—dc21

                                00–037610

ISBN 1 84064 211 4

Printed in the United Kingdom at the University Press, Cambridge

Contents

List of figures

List of tables

Acknowledgments

This book is based on a research project, 'New Networks, New Agendas: Social Environmental Research in the European Union', which was funded by the European Commission's Directorate-General for Science, Research and Development (DGXII: Reference No. ENVU CT96 0190) and coordinated by Michael Redclift. Assistance in writing Chapter 2 was provided by Pirkko Kasanen, in Chapter 3 by Alfredo Cadenas and Pablo del Rio, in Chapter 4 by Liana Giorgi and in Chapter 5 by Heide Hackmann. The authors would also like to acknowledge Debbie Adams, Jose Andringa, Joseph Lekakis, Will Medd, Chris Pantzios and Roman Tronner for their contributions to the research.

Contributors

Alfredo Cadenas is Professor of Economics, Department of Economics, Autonomous University, Madrid, Spain.

Liana Giorgi is Vice-Director of the Interdisciplinary Centre for Comparative Research in the Social Sciences (ICCR), Vienna, Austria.

Heide Hackmann is a researcher in the Centre for Studies of Science, Technology and Society, University of Twente, The Netherlands.

Pirkko Kasanen is Research Director, Department of Home Economics, TTS Work Efficiency Institute, Helsinki, Finland.

Sujatha Raman is a researcher in the Centre for Science Studies, University of Lancaster, UK.

Michael Redclift is Professor of Human Geography and the Environment, Department of Geography, King's College, London, UK.

Pablo del Rio is a lecturer in the Department of Economics, Castilla la Mancha, Spain.

Elizabeth Shove is Director of the Centre for Science Studies, University of Lancaster, UK.

Barend van der Meulen is Senior Researcher, Centre for Studies of Science, Technology and Society, University of Twente, The Netherlands.

1. Researching European social environmental research

INTRODUCTION

The origins of this book provide a good illustration of what it is about. In 1994, Michael Redclift and Elizabeth Shove attended a workshop at which proposals were solicited for the EU's programme on socioeconomic environmental research (SEER). Over dinner that evening, they sketched the first draft of a comparative project on relationships between national and European social environmental research. Subsequently, they selected possible partners from their own interdisciplinary networks, discussed their ideas with these future collaborators, and managed to get a proposal in to Brussels just before the deadline. The project was funded and the first meeting arranged. From the perspective of the SEER programme, a new project team was formed linking people from social environmental research and science policy studies, linking six different countries, stimulating new intellectual interests, affecting individual careers and realizing the EU programme manager's ambitions through coordinated but nonetheless local research activity.

A more detailed analysis of the project and the worlds of which it is a part would show how the ideas outlined in the proposal represented a specific inter-pretation of the mission of the EU programme, and how those ideas were successively translated in the process of actually doing the research. It would show how Michael Redclift, then coordinator of the UK Economic and Social Research Council's (ESRC) Global Environmental Change programme, spanned national and international research communities, and, through this project, created new linkages between UK and EU research programmes. The project's biography would reveal how it became part of the social environ-mental research landscape in Greece, a landscape which was itself the subject of study. It would also highlight the many occasions on which elements of the research were smuggled, like cuckoos' eggs, into other projects and workshops, so creating new connections and ambiguous identities. As might be expected of a complex European project, the practicalities of coordination were planned and structured in terms of clearly defined milestones and deliverables, yet its daily life also reflected working practices of individual project partners which were difficult to control. And last but not least, those involved made linkages not only with policy processes in general, but with actual policy makers on the ground. From time to time, they even found that they were doing some policy making themselves.

We need not take this navel-gazing exercise further to make the point that the research process in which we (Debbie Adams, Jose Andringa, Alfredo Cadenas, Pablo del Rio, Liana Giorgi, Heide Hackmann, Pirkko Kasanen, Joseph Lekakis, Will Medd, Chris Pantzios, Sujatha Raman, Michael Redclift, Elizabeth Shove, Roman Tronner and Barend van der Meulen) were engaged, reflected, though on a smaller scale, the dynamics of the social environmental research we studied and, generalizing further, the dynamics of much other international research activity.

The chapters which follow explore the making of international social science, and the parts which researchers, policy makers and research managers play in creating European social environmental research. This first chapter puts that exploration in context, introducing the core themes of the book and explaining how we approached the challenge of understanding the development and production of social environmental research within and between European member states. In the process, we make use of a variety of conceptual and methodological tools, following the careers of individual researchers, documenting the characteristics of national and international research systems, and reviewing the evolution of organizing concepts and environmental research agendas. The resulting narrative reflects the multidisciplinary backgrounds of its authors, and the dual ambition of contributing to research and science policy as well as to the social analysis of environmental issues. In weaving these interests together the book engages with different audiences.

Fellow social environmental researchers will, for instance, recognize themselves in the pages that follow and in our descriptions of the motivations, priorities and practices which define this field. For these readers we provide a social and political perspective on the daily lives and intellectual preoccupations of academics and others involved in producing environmental social science. Read as a study of the production of policy-relevant research at the European level, the book has much to say about the dynamics of international social science. In presenting and analysing a complex picture of overlapping institutional interests, we go beyond the description of national research systems to develop new models with which to capture the transnational interaction of researchers and funding agencies. In this respect, we engage with issues at the heart of present-day research and science policy. What does it mean to manage an international research programme, and what are the characteristics of international research and science policy?

At the same time, this volume is about the substance and content of social environmental research. By following the flow of resources, researchers and ideas we trace the evolution of organizing concepts which have the power to structure and coordinate research and policy agendas. Questions about the interface between social science and environmental policy are never far away, providing a constant point of reference for readers interested in the framing and management of current environmental problems.

Though these and other readings are possible, the central themes are clear: how has European social environmental research evolved; how does social environmental research relate to policy, and how do national and international research networks, agendas and funders interact?

The next sections of the present chapter position these questions in terms of European environmental policy and the recent history of social environmental research. We then consider the practical and intellectual challenges facing European research managers charged with the task of building a community of social researchers willing to engage with a policy-relevant environmental agenda. Having set the scene in this way, we explain how we approached the study of 'new networks', that is, the formation of new international research teams, and of 'new agendas', the formulation of distinctively European research questions.

The strategy of examining national research systems in the UK, the Netherlands, Austria, Finland, Spain and Greece allowed us to develop a comparative analysis of the management and funding of social environmental research. The practical consequences of these formal systems depend on the way individual researchers respond and react. We therefore move to the level of the individual, showing how social science researchers have been drawn into the environmental field in different countries, and what this means for incentives to participate in international research. Rather than offering our own definitions of what constitutes social environmental research, we argue that research agendas provide important insights into the interface between social science and policy. Viewed as 'boundary objects' (Star and Griesemer, 1989), key concepts such as ecological modernization have an important role in organizing and coordinating research activity.

Further analysis of the circulation of ideas, research agendas and resources, and of the part played by other international agencies, such as the Greening of Industry Network, the International Human Dimensions Programme and the European Science Foundation, highlights features of transnational research which require new forms of explanation. For example, how are we to conceptualize the practices of those international researchers who draw on multiple sources of funding and who skilfully piece together their own programmes of national and international projects? Equally, how are we to make sense of interconnections between national and international research agendas and the paradox that research priorities seem to be converging despite the involvement of an increasingly varied cast of institutional actors? By focusing on what happens between as well as within social environmental research initiatives, we describe and analyse the emergence of what we term a *network of networks*: that is, the development of overlapping relationships between researchers, funders and ideas on an international scale. The conclusion that social environmental research is formed within these plural and intersecting institutions has important practical and theoretical implications for research and science policy, for the future of the field itself and for the relationship between social and natural science and policy.

Before elaborating on these themes, we begin by reflecting on the relationship between social science and environmental policy and ask what lies behind the policy need for social, economic, political and cultural analysis.

EUROPEAN ENVIRONMENTAL POLICY AND THE SOCIAL SCIENCES

Environmental policy has become one of the European Union's most prominent domains of action in the 1990s. A host of policy statements, indicators and legislative instruments introduced under the environmental rubric testifies to this. Indeed, shared environmental action and the building of political cohesion and a common market are now seen as synergistic processes (Golub, 1998). The Community's first environmental efforts were primarily intended to ensure that variation in national standards and regulatory procedures did not obstruct free trade and business competition (Liefferink *et al.*, 1995, p. 3): hardly surprising, given the predominantly economic ethos of the time. Yet the EU has clearly made a significant shift, from early attempts to provide a shared but loose framework for national environmental policies towards a position in which the aim is to create a distinctive European platform for formulating such policies (ibid., p. 4).

The translation of natural scientific environmental research into tractable policy problems has been at the heart of this convergence of economic and environmental objectives into an apparently coherent European agenda. However, this construction of policy from science did not happen overnight. Climate change is one prominent area whose history within the EU is worth examining in some detail. A research programme on climatology was set up by the Community in 1979 to understand the nature of human–climate interactions and their potential to produce global climate change (Liberatore, 1994). However, these questions did not represent a priority area for research; nor did they exist at the political level. To begin with they were regarded as 'merely' scientific issues. It was only in the late 1980s that the greenhouse effect came to be placed on the European policy agenda, with the subsequent international

Rio convention in 1992 helping establish it as a crucial issue. Economists, policy analysts and energy technology experts played a crucial role in the translation of the greenhouse effect into a tractable political problem (ibid., p. 195) and thus one deserving further research in order to underpin deliberate policy intervention. Along the way, social scientists have helped provide a framework within which climate change is assessed and have contributed to the development, selection and evaluation of environmental policy making.

The 1987 Brundtland Report set the stage for the development and widespread adoption of the discourse of sustainability, a discourse which also seeks to reconcile environment and the economy. Sustainable development 'seeks to meet the needs and aspirations of the present without compromising the ability to meet those of the future' (World Commission on Environment and Development, 1987, p. 40), a philosophy which the EU has taken the lead in promoting through its Fifth Action Programme. The rendering of such a broad ambition, with its inevitable tensions and lack of detail into elaborate sustainability statements and then, into instrumental strategies, required a sustained process of mediation and translation. Social scientists have been called upon, partly as a result of their own promotional efforts, to respond to this challenge. It is, however, important to recognize the nature of the task involved, and to reflect on the role which social science has been expected to play.

ENVIRONMENTAL SOCIAL SCIENCE

Being bound up with the physics and chemistry of the atmosphere, the oceans and the earth itself, environmental problems have traditionally been seen as problems which lie squarely, even exclusively, within the realm of the natural sciences. Accordingly, the task of assessing the nature of the problem and of designing relevant and appropriate solutions and strategies for the future has largely fallen to natural scientists and engineers. Where social scientists came into the picture at all, their role was to understand and then fill the 'non-technical' gaps which began to appear in what was and in many ways still is an unashamedly science-based agenda.

Following in the wake of natural scientists and engineers, social researchers were invited to help develop appropriate policy instruments, and to understand, and if possible change, those 'human factors' and so-called 'barriers' which seemed to obstruct the effective implementation of proven technologies and measures. Cast in this way, the human dimension was hardly a dimension of the big picture of environmental change at all, but was instead conceptualized as a minor though sometimes critical ingredient in the social engineering of an environmentally sustainable future.

Critiques of this approach began to appear toward the end of the 1980s, partly because such technocratic perspectives were clearly failing to deliver plausible and effective policy strategies. These opened the way for a broader discussion about the role and contribution of the social sciences (Newby, 1991), and for debate within European policy circles and elsewhere, about the possibly wider contribution social theory and philosophy might make to practical programmes for sustainability. New questions appeared on the agenda regarding the cultural and institutional foundation of peoples' environmental attitudes, beliefs and practices and the relationship between possible pathways to sustainability and the routine organization of everyday life. These issues formed the core agenda for discussion at a formative workshop, held in Florence in June 1990, which informed the first call for proposals under a new EU-funded programme on socioeconomic environmental research (SEER).

Having repositioned social environmental research against this much more extensive intellectual backdrop, those involved were able to locate the themes and threads of contemporary debate in terms of long-standing disciplinary preoccupations. Such moves made it possible to trace the roots of environmental social science back to early analyses of the relationship between nature and society or the material underpinning of different cultures. In this way social environmental research, as an emerging discipline, was nonetheless shown to have a respectable intellectual ancestry.

In practice, interest in environmental sustainability resonated first, and perhaps most strongly, amongst social scientific sub-disciplines already concerned with the distribution and management of natural resources, for instance in the context of rural sociology, agricultural economics and development studies. These strands continue to be important, yet the broadening of debate, together with a growing sense that environmental issues represent a really significant social challenge, has drawn others into the frame.

The catalogue of papers and positions represented at international meetings of environmental social scientists is evidence itself of the range of perspectives now brought to bear on environmental themes. Environmentalism as a social movement and the environment as a social problem (Hannigan, 1995); new forms of risk and the environment (Beck, 1995); equity and sustainable development (Redclift, 1987); reconceptualizing relationships with nature (Benton, 1994); environmental economics (Pearce *et al.*, 1989): these have all become legitimate and interesting areas of enquiry. Though some of the ensuing debate has been internal, focusing on what 'the environment' had to offer the intellectual life of the social sciences, new linkages have been formed with policy analysis and practice, and with the natural sciences. The four volumes of *Human Choice and Climate Change*, edited by Steve Rayner and Elizabeth Malone (1998) and the *International Handbook of Environmental Sociology* (Redclift and Woodgate, 1998) represent impressive collections of recent work in the field. Although they may not quite rival the Intergovernmental Panel on Climate Change (IPCC) reviews of the state of the art in the environmental and natural sciences, they surely demonstrate the range and extent of social scientific endeavour over the last decade.

Sometimes inspired by the ambition of informing policy, sometimes enticed by new funding sources or new intellectual challenges, economists, anthropologists, sociologists, political scientists and others have turned their attention to an ever-widening menu of environmental topics. As a result, there is a growing body of theory and evidence, and a European as well as global research community committed to the social analysis of environmental issues. Even so, it is important to remember that 'the environment' has only recently emerged as a theme within national and international research agendas. Insofar as there is a recognizable field of social environmental research, it is very young. One consequence is that definitions are fluid. More than that, levels and forms of institutionalization vary dramatically from one country to another. As we will see in Chapter 2, some countries have supported major programmes of social environmental research while, in others, the social environmental research 'community' consists of a loose coalition of individual researchers and a handful of projects.

This short history presents practical problems for European research managers who have to entice researchers into a substantially new field and encourage them to produce research relevant to the design and implementation of effective environmental policy. The next section describes some of the competing pressures and demands which have influenced the way in which EU-funded research has developed in, and helped to define, this field.

CREATING EUROPEAN SOCIAL ENVIRONMENTAL RESEARCH

The first call for EU-funded SEER was launched in 1991, following a series of workshops, discussions and reviews of the proposed work programme. Responses were invited under four headings: the relationship between the human being and nature; environmental policy implementation and monitoring; environmental problems in an international perspective; and methodological and epistemological (metascientific) research of importance for environmental problems and policies. These themes, designed to generate research which would identify and illuminate 'a continuum of possible transition paths suitable for different regions, nations, religions and social groups', represented a clear invitation to the social sciences. Their help was needed to develop new approaches to the analysis of economic development and environmental costs, to bring a more social and cultural perspective to bear on the shaping of institutional reform and the management of environmental and technological innovation, and to provide useful critiques of established methods, policy assumptions and procedures.

The first 37 projects to be funded under this programme addressed some, but not all, of these themes. Further calls for proposals, each organized around a new work programme, were issued in 1993 and 1996. As we show in Chapter 4, priorities have moved quite significantly over the years. Some features, however, have remained constant. The 1996 work programme of the Human Dimensions element of the Environment and Climate Programme, the successor to SEER (European Commission, 1996) makes it clear that the purpose of research is still to 'improve the basis of policies and actions in support of sustainable development in the EU' (p. 51). This policy orientation, and a corresponding focus on the international, or at least European, dimensions of environmental problems, goes hand-in-hand with a common emphasis on interdisciplinarity. Again, the 1996 work programme underlines the point that both social and natural sciences are required for 'better understanding the processes underlying environmental change'; for 'improving assessment of the consequences of climatic and other environmental change'; for contributing to the 'identification, formulation and implementation of societal policy and technological responses to global environmental change' and for 'developing methodologies for monitoring and warning of environmental hazards'.

These statements and ambitions threw down the gauntlet for European research and science policy. Is it possible to engineer the type of interdisciplinary research or the form of social environmental enquiry which appears to be required? What can programme managers do to stimulate applications and proposals in what seemed to many to be a field with no history and in which relevant research expertise was limited, and unevenly distributed between countries?

Interviews with relevant programme managers in Brussels, and analysis of work programmes and other documentary material, provided a picture of the institutional constraints and opportunities which have a bearing on European research management and on the work which is eventually funded and undertaken.

Our interviews, held in 1998, focused on the design of the Human Dimensions element of the Environment and Climate programme. Rather than seeing the programme as a single-minded actor able to steer researchers and agendas in any way it chooses, we view it, rather, as a system which is itself shaped by linkages with a myriad of other actors, including the research community (acting as suppliers of research, or as peer reviewers and expert advisors), actual and potential research users (for example, other directorates-general, and EU, national, regional and even local policy makers), and national research and policy institutions whose agendas and practices have a bearing on EU objectives and ambitions.

Figure 1.1 shows how EU programme development is positioned by and between these other interests. Those responsible for developing and managing the Human Dimensions programme were caught between competing demands and limited in their ability to respond by virtue of their position at the centre of the triangle and by the internal structures and dynamics of the wider institution in which they are located. The core processes of programme management – the definition of a work programme and the organization of advisory committees; tendering for and selecting proposals and, further down the line, evaluating the programme itself – all have their own conventions and rules, the operation of which depends on other key features such as the number of staff employed and the resources at their disposal.

The fact that EU research programme managers invest so heavily in developing and drafting the work programme suggests that it represents a key instrument for influence. Work programmes are initiated by a small core of people but then subject to rigorous review and comment from a network of national experts, researchers and advisors. The range of stakeholders involved again reminds us of how dependent EU research management is on the input of people who are also key players within their own national contexts.

Having survived the checks and balances of its production, the resulting document becomes a commodity in its own right, circulating between nations and sometimes appropriated wholesale by countries seeking a ready-made

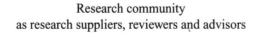

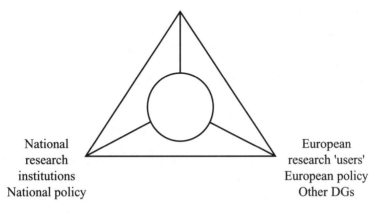

Figure 1.1   The location of European research programmes

research framework which, by definition, tallies with European priorities. Work programmes do more than simply outline important research themes. They also define the extent to which problems are specified in advance and hence bound the scope of response. Opinions differed on this point and on the preferred distribution of responsibility between researcher and programme manager. Some argued that the only way to engender appropriately 'European' research was to ensure that researchers have significant input to the agenda and sufficient scope to interpret it in ways that make sense to them. Others claimed, equally forcefully, that research funds would be better spent if research briefs were closely scripted, tightly defined and precisely directed. This, they argued, was the only way in which programme managers would ever be able to deliver the sort of social science which EU policy makers require. If anything, these debates highlight the pivotal role of researchers, without whom there would be no projects, and no programmes.

The conditions and circumstances of researchers' involvement are therefore especially relevant. Research is expected to add value to the European project by contributing in some way to the promotion of community-wide cohesion. Transnational collaboration is therefore a condition of EU funding, with managers especially keen on bringing in researchers from underrepresented Mediterranean countries. Calls for proposals set in motion a process in which interested researchers search for potential collaborators in other countries. Given the uneven development of social environmental research, this search process is marked by a correspondingly uneven set of incentives for becoming involved. Actual and potential partners' personal and intellectual ambitions reflect their own national experiences and interests. This diversity generates inevitable tensions, not only within project teams but also between researchers' motivations and the ambitions of EU research programme managers. Though committed to delivering relevant and useful research to European and national policy makers, programme research managers do not and cannot control the selection of projects (which depends on peer review) or the flow and content of applications. Adjustments can sometimes be made at the point of contract negotiation but, beyond that, the multinational research teams are very much in charge.

There are two points to note here. One is the successive evolution and informal renegotiation and reshaping of the original (thoroughly reviewed) work programme. Once released to the research community, those key pages take on a life of their own, being subject to selective reading and interpretation in the structuring of proposals, in their evaluation and selection, and in the way that research is subsequently undertaken and managed. In very simple terms, the programme determines the profile of those who participate in it, but it is the participants who give content to the programme itself.

A second feature of this situation is that EU research programme managers have no way of retrospectively filling what are agreed to be important gaps in the resulting research portfolio. They can offer informal advice and encouragement, and do what they can to spark interest and inspire and stimulate research proposals in what they take to be key areas, but they are simply unable to 'force' projects or project teams into existence, or ensure interaction between disciplines. However strong the demand, the supply of particular sorts of environmental social science research cannot be guaranteed.

None of this detracts from the achievements of the SEER and the Human Dimensions programmes. Having started in what was perceived to be a 'new' area, and thus having confronted the challenge of generating research interest from 'scratch', the Human Dimensions programme has been able to measure its success by the number of good quality applications it attracts, and by the range of research institutes and individuals willing to invest time and energy in preparing proposals and pursuing research in this field.

The process of building a programme has a narrative of its own, but one which is also closely related to the expectations which others have of what it can and should deliver. Again, EU research programme managers find themselves mediating between contrasting views of social science and its relevance to the environmental policy process. Several respondents (within the Directorate-General for Environment, Nuclear Safety and Civil Protection, DGXI, and the Directorate-General for Science, Research and Development, DGXII) subscribed to the view that social science research was urgently needed in three areas: in developing indicators of sustainable development, evaluating policy instruments (taxation, regulation and so on) and providing up-to-date intelligence about people's environmental values. The difficulty is that, if the Human Dimensions programme were to limit itself to this rather narrowly defined agenda, it might fail to inspire or support the sort of research required not just now but also in the future.

To summarize, our interviews highlighted the existence of layers of quasi-research users each claiming to 'know' what policy makers really want and each striving to ensure that research agendas reflect these second- or third-hand perceptions of the sorts of data, arguments, intelligence and research capacity 'really' required. The role and influence of 'users' is further complicated by the time scales involved and the years which pass between the development of a work programme and the delivery of the research it promised. Meanwhile, the canvas of policy interests is constantly on the move.

This brief description illustrates some of the relationships, tensions and conditions which have shaped the definition and management of EU-funded social environmental research and which have led, thus far, to the involvement of 558 researchers from 25 different countries, as either project partners or project coordinators. Many more people are, of course, involved as research assistants or as PhD students working on topics related to EU-funded projects.

In describing the context of SEER and the Human Dimensions research programme, we have outlined the characteristics of European research management as if that represented a world in its own right. In reality, European-level research initiatives are doubly looped into national practices: not only are they shaped, undertaken and managed by researchers who are also part of a national research environment, they also feed back and in turn influence events within those national settings.

EXPLORING NEW NETWORKS AND NEW AGENDAS

In the chapters which follow we explore different aspects of this phenomenon, not with a view to evaluating the successes or failures of the EU programme, but with the aim of understanding the creation of social environmental research through an analysis of the actions and interactions of researchers, funders and policy makers within national and international contexts. Two questions guided our enquiry: (a) how do national research environments influence the formation of European social environmental research networks and agendas, and, (b) how do European programmes influence national practices and agendas in the field of social environmental research?

These core concerns led us to focus on flows of people (that is, research capacity), resources (including money but also reputation and other forms of social capital) and ideas (that is, the agendas and questions to which social environmental scientists attend) within and between national and international research environments. It also led us to concentrate on the social and institutional dynamics involved in making new networks and new agendas. New networks involve the formation and operation of transnational project teams involving researchers each of whom is anchored in a different national system and tradition. Looking further ahead, we ask whether there is such a thing as a European social environmental research community with its own identity and characteristics. New agendas are the formulation of a distinctively European set of social environmental concerns, again drawing from and feeding back into national agendas and relating, in different ways, to national and international environmental policy.

In the next section we explain how we put the above aims into practice, and describe the methodological strategies and conceptual tools we adopted in the course of undertaking a project which was itself funded under the Human Dimensions of Environmental Change programme.

RESEARCHING SOCIAL ENVIRONMENTAL RESEARCH

Students of science and research policy have invested considerable effort in characterizing and describing national research systems (Cozzens *et al.*, 1990; van der Meulen and Rip, 1998; Wagner *et al.*, 1991; Wittrock and Elzinga, 1985). Given our interest in the relationship between national and European networks and agendas, it made sense to draw on this work and begin by building up a picture of the institutional structure, organization and funding of social environmental research in different European countries.

In developing a research design which would allow us to compare national research systems, we made a number of important assumptions. First, we assumed that we would be able to identify and describe instances of social environmental research, and that we could plot and then review the distribution of social environmental researchers and the unfolding of social environmental research agendas country by country. Second, we hoped to detect and so track relationships between the trajectories of social environmental research at the European level and within individual countries. In other words, we hoped to reveal patterns of mutual influence between these two 'layers'. This ambition informed the selection of the six countries on which we focused.

Two countries, the UK and the Netherlands, had a relatively long tradition of social environmental research. Both had organized research programmes in this field as well as a history of active involvement at the EU level. By contrast, social environmental research barely existed as a recognizable activity within Spain and Greece, though both countries had extensive experience of participation in EU research and development programmes. Despite being new entrants to the EU, Austria and Finland already had a history of supporting social environmental research. This combination of countries permitted various lines of comparative analysis, for instance, between Northern and Southern Europe, between countries which did and did not have national social environmental research programmes and between those which were and were not familiar with the bureaucracy of EU research.

With this comparative framework in place, we sought to describe relevant features of national systems, showing how social environmental research was funded and how research agendas related to policy. This involved us in mapping the role and function of key institutions and plotting relationships between research funders and research providers, including relevant institutes, centres, universities and consultants.

Though useful in its own right, this institutional analysis failed to reveal the ambitions and aspirations of researchers on the ground. In order to learn more about the way these formal systems influenced the shaping of social environmental networks and agendas, we had to get closer to the individuals involved. Interviews with researchers who were part of EU programmes or who were responsible for nationally funded social environmental research projects revealed their motivations for becoming involved and provided important insights into the otherwise obscure process of forming and managing international project teams. National data on projects and project participants also demonstrated, albeit rather more distantly, the practical consequences of research funding regimes and the incentives associated with them.

Analysis of catalogues listing SEER and Human Dimensions of Environmental Change projects and participants involved provided further insights into the range of researchers drawn into the programme. We combined this material, together with similar published data from other international programmes, into a single database of individuals and institutions involved in national and European social environmental research. We draw on this resource in Chapters 2 and 3, using it to identify key figures in the international research network, and to reveal what we term *serial operators*, that is, individuals who have received funding from several different research programmes in the field.

Investigation of institutional and individual 'levels' of research activity showed how national systems worked, but did not get us very far in terms of understanding the substance of social environmental research. Which issues came to the fore, why, and what politics of knowledge lay behind the unfolding of national, let alone international agendas? Content analysis of calls for proposals, work programmes and other documents allowed us to observe the flow of environmental issues between research programmes and between the EU and the six member states we examined. Putting these lines, or 'levels', of enquiry together, we construct a 'layered' analysis of the mutual shaping of national and European research agendas and research networks, as illustrated in Figure 1.2.

Although this model of interacting layers – the European, the national, and the individual – generated interesting results, it did not, and perhaps could not, account for the dynamics of the process we observed, or for the distinctive characteristics of international research relationships. Much of what we discovered fell outside this framework.

To give just a few examples, it became clear that certain researchers simultaneously exploited different sources of funding. They were quite precisely attuned to the relative costs and benefits of pursuing funding from national sources, from the EU, or from other international agencies, and organized their research effort accordingly. The conventions of these funding games did vary between countries and did, in part, depend on the operation of national research systems. Where national research resources were scarce, researchers were more inclined to bid for European projects. Equally, some national governments (for example, Finland) 'rewarded' those who succeeded in securing European money by providing them with additional national funding. Such variations might be expected. What came as a surprise was the extent to which researchers

Figure 1.2   The 'layers' of European research agendas and networks

traded between national and international agencies, playing one off against the other and using resources from one funder to gain leverage elsewhere. In other words, this was not a matter of one source or 'layer' of funding replacing another, but of an increasingly complex 'market' populated by an increasing number of funders and research providers.

A similarly complex picture emerged when we enquired into the daily lives of individual researchers and questioned them about their social environmental research careers. Again the layered model simply failed to capture the way in which researchers and research groups simultaneously managed their own portfolios of projects, often relying on studentships, advice and consultancy work as well as on more conventional forms of research funding. In this way they assembled hybrid careers, pursuing their own agendas through a mixture of apparently discrete projects, the real purpose of which was frequently unknown to those sponsoring individual elements of the total patchwork. In this overlapping environment it was both possible and sensible to promote and develop 'the same' piece of work in different ways for different audiences or funders, and in the process build up an identity and a reputation across a variety of research networks.

We might still describe these practices in terms of movements between a 'layered', or tiered, research community, yet that would be to miss the point that national and international research communities are populated by the same people wearing different hats on different occasions. Rather than weaving between distinct research environments, experienced researchers in fact spend their time weaving them together.

Further reflection on the activities of funding agencies (both national and international) suggests that they are also party to a more fluid and interactive enterprise than the layered model would suggest. There is, for instance, some evidence to suggest that Greek social environmental research priorities are modelled on those outlined in the latest EU work programmes. On the other hand, the EU research agenda is itself strongly influenced by the ideas, priorities and environmental policy programmes of Northern European countries (such as the UK and the Netherlands) which are used to providing EU research managers with advice, consultancy and input. Rather than observing a two-way flow between national and European levels, we see a more elaborate interweaving of agendas and priorities in which the EU is positioned as one amongst other players. This is even more evident when we recall that the EU is only one of several international organizations concerned to promote social environmental research. This realization prompted us to consider the ambitions and characteristics of other European research actors, such as the Greening of Industry Network, the European Science Foundation's Tackling Environmental Resource Management and the International Human Dimensions Programme, to see what part they played in shaping the field.

The results confirmed the sense that research funders were also locked into networks of overlapping and interdependent relationships. Though their work is often guided by quite different rules and ambitions (to add European value, to encourage young researchers, to improve EU policy making, to support networking but not research, or research but not networking, and so on), it is clearly the case that European players depend on research capacity and sometimes also on research funding which has been generated elsewhere in the system.

The 'layered' model suggests that the subjects and issues which constitute the substance of social environmental research are forged through interaction and more or less explicit negotiation between researchers, funders and policy makers or users at different levels. An alternative perspective, and one which better fits the evidence we have, understands the circulation of ideas in terms of their ability (or otherwise) to provide a common point of reference, or the illusion of one, for the many different interests implicated in the research and funding networks described above. Borrowing the concept from science and technology studies, it makes sense to see research agendas as 'boundary objects', that is, as entities or ideas which different parties recognize and relate to and which make interaction possible despite the fact that interests and interpretations only partly overlap.

As these observations suggest, the layered model, the polarizing language of national and European research systems, and even our own comparative framework obscured the processes and dynamics of European social environmental research. We therefore looked for other concepts better suited to the task. In constructing an alternative model – a 'network of networks' – we sought to capture the circulation of ideas, money and people not simply between national and international levels, but within overlapping networks.

Having outlined the questions which lie at the heart of the book, and the means by which we address them, we now provide an overview of the chapters which follow.

CHAPTER 2

We knew from the start that only some countries had formal programmes for social environmental research, and that possibilities for state or central steering of activity in this area would vary accordingly. Taking a step back, our aim in this chapter is to characterize and delineate relevant features of national systems: to show where social environmental research lies within the research landscape, how it is funded, what strings are attached and how loose or close the links are between researchers and policy. This is a macro level of investigation which involves plotting institutions, identifying key players such as research councils, government departments and research producers, and examining how these different units relate to each other. Against this institutional context, we are particularly interested in mapping specific efforts made to encourage social environmental research, the form they took and the reasons for their introduction.

Following an overview of social environmental research in each of our six countries (Austria, Greece, Finland, Spain, the Netherlands and the UK) we provide a comparative analysis in terms of four key variables: national research capacity, the extent of national programme development, national level of competition for research funding, and patterns of interaction between research and policy. Each of these factors not only gives a particular shape to the national research system itself, but also influences the way in which it interacts with research institutions at the European level.

CHAPTER 3

Interviews with a sample of researchers involved in both national and European-funded social environmental research projects gave us access to the ways in which national systems had effect on the ground. Social environmental research is a new and sub-disciplinary area which remains on the margins of activity in recognized social science disciplines. So, we asked, what were the motivations for becoming involved? Were there systematic patterns in terms of researchers' age, or background and personal history? How did individuals with a diversity of incentives link up to form project teams? More simply, how did they even find each other?

In exploring these questions from the individual perspective, we also take note of the formation of what seems to be a new elite at the European level. Research 'barons' or 'serial operators' have been in the midst of this new area from early on. Already equipped with a network of friends and colleagues in other countries, they have been able to claim and subsequently develop expertise in the field of social environmental research. On this basis they have sometimes steered research and policy agendas in directions of their own making. We contrast these experiences with those of research assistants who have to negotiate a more uncertain and unstable set of options.

CHAPTER 4

What individuals get drawn into is a part-product of national agenda/priority setting and a part-product of the way they respond to invitations to tender and to calls for research proposals. For instance, linkages with environmental policy depend, in different countries, on the way that policy is itself managed and on the extent to which it exists as a discrete activity. More loosely, interpretations of what is relevant about the environment differ in ways that are not entirely unrelated to distributions of natural resources and related interpretations of more or less pressing environmental problems. To give just a couple of examples, the environment is frequently equated with natural resource management in Finland and Spain, with ecological modernization and clean technology in the Netherlands, and in social science research terms, with global rather than local issues in the UK, but with local rather than global questions in Austria.

The evolution of the EU research agenda can only be understood with reference to national interpretations and practices which it either contradicts or enhances. As we show, ideas and priorities flow unevenly between national and European levels. Developing this theme, we argue that the European agenda in social environmental research has, after its beginnings in some fairly broad expectations, converged around a rather technocratic focus on policy tools. In particular, the discourse of ecological modernization, which claims to reconcile the objectives of environmental improvement with economic growth, has been very influential in shaping research. Drawing on the concept of 'boundary objects' in the sociology of science, we attempt to explain how such a narrowing of the European research agenda can be seen even amidst the multiplicity of interests, approaches and disciplinary and national backgrounds which researchers bring to this emerging field.

CHAPTER 5

In this chapter we take note of the fact that the EU is not the only institutional actor in the domain of European social environmental research. Rather, the EU's programme exists in a double market of funding and ideas and as such competes for attention alongside other international initiatives also concerned with the human dimensions of environmental change.

We review accounts of routine research practice and reflect on the routes through which projects and people come together. These sometimes chaotic narratives show how formalized programmes of funding and research management work out on the ground, and how individual researchers respond to the multiple, sometimes overlapping, opportunities generated by the intersection of social environmental research and policy initiatives.

Analyses couched in the rather static terms of national or international research systems failed to explain the practices and relationships we observed. A new model and a new frame of reference were required if we were to represent the flows of ideas, people and resources which constitute European social environmental research. The concept of a 'network of networks' fits this bill and allows us to capture at least some of the dynamics of international research activity.

CHAPTER 6

The final chapter considers first the implications of these ideas and insights for the substance of social environmental research. Successive calls for proposals reveal a steady narrowing of the social environmental research agenda and a somewhat restrictive interpretation of the potential role and contribution of the social sciences with respect to natural science and policy. Chapters 4 and 5 explain this process, first, in terms of the unifying potential of shared concepts such as that of ecological modernization, and then with reference to the effect of mutual reinforcement generated by overlapping networks of multiple national and international funding agencies. In Chapter 6 we ask what these tendencies mean for the possibility of a more critical and a more challenging form of social environmental enquiry.

Our second concluding theme concerns the relationship between research and policy. European social environmental research was, from the start, designed to influence policy; yet our work suggests that agendas and practices are organized around second-hand notions of what policy makers want, rather than first-hand experiences of research in use. The circulation of seemingly shared concepts and themes plays an important part in creating and sustaining a sense of policy relevance, but in practice there are few mechanisms for engendering serious and sustained interaction between social environmental research and policy.

Chapter 6 then highlights implications and conclusions for international research and science policy. Having moved away from a language of national and international research systems, and having more or less abandoned the notion that research managers are in a position singlehandedly to set research agendas, we ask the question, what does it mean to make or implement international research policy? What positions do research funders occupy within the interlocking networks of networks which we describe? We argue that research dynamics revolve around circulation and accumulation of people, ideas and money, and suggest that funders' and researchers' practices are closely related, if not wholly interdependent. It is in this context that research agendas and networks, not just of researchers, but of funders and policy makers too, have an active and continuing part to play in the coordination of research activity.

2. Social environmental research at the national level

INTRODUCTION

The previous chapter set out the reasons for undertaking research into research on the environment – a form of 'meta research'. In the present chapter and the two that follow we examine the principal dimensions of that activity: the institutions and structures within which social environmental research is undertaken; the strategies and careers of individual researchers; and the ideas and research agendas which have provided the content of research networks.

We should begin by outlining the reasons for looking closely at the institutions and structures within which research is undertaken at the national level, in the six countries we studied. This chapter examines European research on the environment by reviewing research at the national level, both in dedicated research 'programmes' and in other forms of activity. It demonstrates that the way in which research is organized, and the institutions which 'steer' research, contribute to national research capacity and, at the same time, influence the way in which individuals and groups of researchers become involved in European-level research on the environment. It examines the level of institutionalization of social environmental research by analysing the organizations responsible for research within individual countries. In some cases, leading organizations are government departments. In others, they are research councils, acting with some degree of autonomy. In still others, they are institutions of higher education, private foundations or industrial corporations. We locate these different institutional arrangements within a configuration representative of each national case.

A major finding of our research is the existence of specifically European networks and practices that are more than the sum of national systems. In this context, we might expect that national research systems would have to change and adapt themselves in response to European Community-led factors, in turn transforming their structures. Our descriptions of each national case pay specific attention to the role of this influence.

The national experiences of social environmental research discussed in this book were chosen to reflect a number of different variables. These criteria included 'northern' and 'southern' European emphases in research; the extent to which national programmes of research had developed; the length of time for which individual countries have fully participated in EU-wide research; and the emphasis placed on directed research to meet policy needs rather than responsive research which largely reflects the interests of the research community.

Research programmes, and particularly those in new and emerging areas such as the environment, require more than the appearance of research activity, and the identification of new research priorities. They also need at least an outline research agenda, followed by active research commissioning, management and evaluation. They need researchers, people ready to manage and organize their research and, increasingly, a clearly identifiable group of 'users' of research or those who might benefit from it. Throughout the process of agenda setting in which research programmes are developed and research is commissioned, choices are made which influence the character and likely outcome of these new research initiatives.

Having examined the extent to which programmes have developed through different institutions, and the relationships between these institutions, the chapter then explores the extent to which social environmental research programmes, in their content and intention, reflect existing research priorities, or seek to establish new ones. The bigger the 'steer' given to research, the more it usually seeks to encourage research which is of use to policy. Given that programmes may act as devices for shaping academic agendas, this way of characterizing research also allows us to explore linkages between policy-relevant research and the utility of some steering devices. It helps us to gain knowledge about the degree of success achieved by very different research systems and cultures in pursuing their agendas.

Finally, this chapter briefly relates the nature of institutionalization of research at the national level to that at the level of the European Union. It examines whether national strategies for promoting greater participation in EU-led research vary according to different modes and levels of institutionalization. The focus on research programmes concentrates on their possible role as devices for responding to EU research opportunities, or as a means of increasing research capacity throughout Europe: for example, by helping train new generations of researchers who operate within a Europe-wide market for research.

In the following section we introduce an analytical framework for investigating national research systems. The chapter then considers some of the ways in which this framework helps us understand national systems better.

ANALYSING NATIONAL RESEARCH SYSTEMS: CONCEPTUAL AND METHODOLOGICAL PROBLEMS

In discussing national research systems from a comparative perspective, we are faced with a number of important conceptual and methodological problems. The analytical framework outlined in the next section helps us tackle some of them.

- Descriptions of national research systems usually concentrate on their formal organization, rather than the way in which these systems work. Institutions such as research councils frequently function differently in different research cultures; their way of working needs to be related to the specific culture and configuration of institutions, such as government departments, research councils, business organizations and non-governmental organizations, in each specific national case. By focusing on institutional structures, we are able to map the specific configurations of organizations involved in funding or undertaking research.
- Knowledge of the institutional structure of each national research system does not, in itself, enable us to compare their management or organization, or to compare how social environmental research is funded. By considering the normative and pragmatic rules which govern the way they work, we can better appreciate the way in which national structures facilitate (or prevent) international collaboration in environmental research.
- The language and terminology that are used to describe research systems are not consistent between national cases. For example, the terms 'basic' and 'applied' research are used in different ways within different national research systems. In Spain, 'basic' research is research that has been independently refereed or subject to peer review. In other countries, such as the United Kingdom, basic or 'blue skies' research is research that has not been significantly influenced by policy considerations. The issue is not whether the research is subject to external peer review but the extent to which its design is 'freed' from the need to be practically useful or policy-relevant. Other similar examples could be quoted, such as the sense in which a research system is 'steered' by its managers. This is frequently understood quite differently in different countries.
- A central paradox uncovered by this research is the following. There appears to be a *convergence in the priorities of European social environmental research*, at the national as well as the European level, while *research cultures and institutions in each country are often radically different*. Our framework suggests that this may be because the formal structures to which researchers and research managers adhere are sometimes little more than a camouflage for informal connections which activate personal networks and change research agendas.

ANALYSING NATIONAL RESEARCH SYSTEMS: AN INSTITUTIONAL FRAMEWORK

In order to analyse how organizational structures and research cultures are linked, we can borrow some analytical tools from the institutionalist literature in social science (DiMaggio and Powell, 1991) and from studies of national innovation systems (Lundvall, 1992; Nelson, 1993). As in previous work on national research systems (Cozzens *et al.*, 1990), we are concerned with patterns of research organization and knowledge exchange that underpin the development of new fields of inquiry. 'Products' of innovation, in this case, are such things as research grants, reports, new ideas and enhanced human capacity.

We employ three main concepts to understand the different national configurations of social environmental research in Europe.

1. *Institutional structures* are the structures of research in each case, best regarded as dynamic and evolving within the broader confines of the European Union.
2. *Normative and pragmatic rules* are those rules that govern the behaviour of groups and individuals operating within these research structures.
3. *Structural transformation* refers to modifications in national research systems which are prompted, and made possible, by social environmental research at the level of the European Union.

We begin by examining *institutional structures*. The research systems with which we are dealing are each made up of different organizations, each with different internal traditions and ways of behaviour. The pattern of linkage and interaction between the organizations that make up a system is what may be called an institutional structure. In examining national systems from such a standpoint, 'we are seeking a level of understanding of how the game works which may not be known to those who play it' (Bailey, 1969, p. 9): in other words, an outsider's view of the way different parts link up. We are concerned not only with what formal organizations (the government departments, research councils and universities) think they are doing, but with their mutual relationships with research communities and research cultures. As Bailey reminds us, 'structures *interact* with their environments: the arrows of causation point in both directions' (ibid., p. 11).

The second analytical distinction of importance concerns the way in which people and groups function within research systems: the rules that drive their institutional practices (DiMaggio and Powell, 1991). As Bailey puts it, 'in any culture, there are regular and accepted ways of getting things done and of prevailing over others; ... actions have a determinate range of consequences; ... and the actors in any particular culture believe they know what these consequences are' (Bailey, 1969, p. xiii). So national research systems exhibit different levels of research competition, depending on their level of resources and human capacity. That is, there are certain rules laid out by institutional structures that enable, constrain and generally shape the behaviour of researchers within the system in question. Rules implicitly identify and circumscribe those courses of action which are deemed to be appropriate and which might expect to be rewarded. There are two forms of rule governing institutional structures: *normative rules* and *pragmatic rules*. The normative rules of national research systems prescribe the range of actions required for researchers to gain funds and resources. However, as researchers reach beyond the national arena and into the European institution, these boundaries may begin to be breached.

The Work Programmes of the European Commission's Directorate-General XII (Science, Research and Development), provide the formal set of normative rules for researchers operating at the European level. However, they do not tell players how to actually interpret and apply these rules. Further, more informal directives come into existence to help fill the 'empty spaces' left by the texts of research programmes or initiatives. A set of pragmatic rules therefore emerge as players, in teams and as individuals, manoeuvre within the wider research system and construct their tactics on the ground. Pragmatic rules 'are statements not about whether a particular line of conduct is just or unjust, but about whether or not it will be effective' (ibid., p. 6). In focusing on the motivation and behaviour of individual researchers, Chapter 3 draws on this concept.

While, at any one time, institutional structures may protect themselves by dis-qualifying whole classes of potential players from competing for research funds, there is always the possibility that new organizations will develop and thereby force a change in rules. The rise of private environmental consultancies is an example in this context; they have come to rival existing public and academic institutions, and are 'waiting to take the job over' from them (ibid., p. 11). Most of the national cases we explore below consist of combinations of different organizations whose structural relationship has been changing, most markedly under the influence of new resources from the European Union.

Finally, from an analytical perspective, *structural transformation* refers to the process and outcome of change in institutional structures. As both nation states and the European Union come to assume different levels of resource allocation ('resources' here being research projects and grants), the distinction between normative and pragmatic rules becomes important. Structural changes occur when the relationship between the rules governing behaviour in systems comes into conflict. As a new line of enquiry which crosses existing research frontiers and boundaries, social environmental research causes a disturbance of sorts in the system and calls for the development of new institutional agendas. We will see in Chapter 4 that the idea of 'ecological modernization' is, arguably, beginning to fill this role by claiming that environmental objectives and economic imperatives can be reconciled with each other.

The analytical framework above can also be extended to the international level where we can observe a 'network of networks', or overlapping relation-ships between researchers, funders and ideas flowing into and out of different countries. The dynamic and interactive dimensions of this process will be elaborated upon in Chapters 5 and 6.

NATIONAL RESEARCH SYSTEMS: AN OVERVIEW OF THEIR DEVELOPMENT

At the national level in Europe, there are three principal types of organization with an interest in the promotion of social environmental research: *research councils, government departments* (serving as both funders and users of research) and the *community of researchers* themselves. In the analysis undertaken in this chapter we observe that the balance struck between each of these three institutional actors makes a difference to the way in which research programmes are (or are not) defined and managed. We begin, then, by focusing on these three groups in shaping research programmes and in undertaking, promoting and utilizing the research.

This kind of comparative exercise necessarily involves playing down some otherwise important differences: for example, what is meant by a 'research council' varies in each case, sometimes quite significantly, from one country to the next. Similarly, different meanings are attached to the terms 'basic' and 'applied' research, as we saw above. In the interests of emphasizing comparison, we have had to ignore some of the variation in the way these terms are used at the national level.

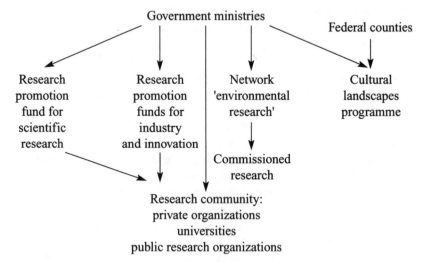

Figure 2.1   Social environmental research in Austria

With these qualifications in mind, we now present an overview of the social environmental research system in each of the six countries studied: Austria, Greece, Spain, Finland, the Netherlands and the United Kingdom.

Until the early 1990s, Austrian research on environmental issues was formulated largely on an ad hoc basis in response to specific policy challenges. The proliferation of commissioned studies on problems associated with acid rain is indicative of the nature of the policy–research relationship. With research tied closely to the specific requirements of different government departments, fragmentation was typical in most research areas, not merely the social environmental one. Environmental research was funded not only by the Austrian Federal Ministry of the Environment but also by three other ministries. Thus, the pattern was one of fragmentation in both substance (the nature of issues addressed) and location (the organizational context in which research was done).

By 1990, however, Austria had developed a National Environmental Plan. This provided the impetus to a greater integration of research related to environmental policy. A comprehensive approach was developed in conjunction with researchers and users. In this context, the role of interdisciplinary work, as well as of the social sciences, began to be recognized. This, in turn, was linked to Austria's accession to the European Union in 1995, which intensified the orientation towards global issues. With new expectations about its usefulness, social environmental research expanded, not only in terms of funding, but also in the scope of its content. From being largely about relatively narrow technical questions framed around 'end-of-pipe' technologies in the 1970s, social environmental research began to take on more integrated work on sustainable development in the 1990s, thus becoming more closely linked with wider, international concerns (see Figure 2.1).

A key sign of the shift from a problem-driven ad hoc approach is the emergence of two new institutional arrangements, both initiated by the Federal Ministry for Science, Research and the Arts as part of its effort to coordinate research for Austrian involvement in the EU's Fourth Framework Programme. One is the network, SUSTAIN, whose aim is to coordinate research on the environment across the country and improve the flow of information between researchers and public authorities. Set up in 1995, SUSTAIN specifically includes the theme of 'social environmental research' alongside eight other nodes of activity. A second node, on 'cultural landscapes', also contains some work that could be seen as social environmental in nature. 'Cultural landscapes' is also the theme of the Science Ministry's other new arrangement, a research programme introduced in 1992. While devoted to environmental problems in the Danube and Alpine areas, this programme encourages interdisciplinarity and therefore has a place for social scientists.

Finally, the relatively new Austrian Institute for Sustainability (OIN) is yet another location in which social environmental research has come to flourish in light of an explicitly interdisciplinary agenda. Set up in 1995 at the University of Agriculture in Vienna, OIN's mission is to promote sustainable development by carrying out applied research and organizing various exchanges between policy, research and regional actors.

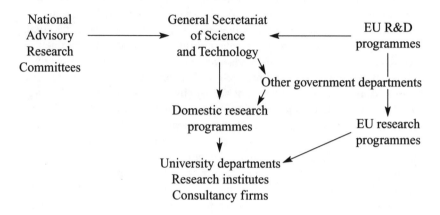

Figure 2.2   Social environmental research in Greece

Primarily administered by government bodies, the research system in Greece (see Figure 2.2) is heavily problem-driven. With individuals limited to responding to periodic calls from various departments in a context of generally scarce funding, the scope for integrated environmental research is even less than in pre-1990s Austria. Indeed, prior to the 1980s, social environmental research was effectively non-existent – the environment-related work that was commissioned came entirely from the natural sciences and engineering.

Since the early 1980s, some social environmental research has been undertaken. Though it remains very limited in comparison with other countries, the fact that it has even taken off is closely linked to the process of European integration. Currently, the largest proportion of total research funding across all areas is provided by the European Union. In turn, national research priorities are being set to reflect the inflow and availability of EU funds. Hence work commissioned by government bodies closely parallels the Framework Programmes.

Within European Community-funded environmental research, the EU's structural funds designated for 'less developed' areas (the so-called 'Objective 1 regions') is an important resource in conjunction with the more transparently European Framework Programme work. Some research is also undertaken on a bilateral basis with other countries, many of them also EU members.

In all, Greek environmental research is overwhelmingly oriented towards the natural sciences. There is no sign of the social sciences in the domestic projects commissioned by the Ministry of Environment, Physical Planning and Public Works. Further, of all EU-funded projects with Greek partners, social environmental projects represent only 6 per cent.

It has been estimated that only about 10 per cent of total EU research funds goes to the poorest countries, with 40 per cent of the population. The research gap between economically well endowed countries and the poorer areas in southern Europe has therefore been exacerbated, although structural funds initiatives are attempting to alleviate the situation. On the other hand, environmental research and policy in southern Europe naturally reflect greater attention to 'development' issues such as water scarcity or environmental health than to the global environment per se. The social environmental research system in Greece (and in Spain, examined next) must necessarily be seen in this context.

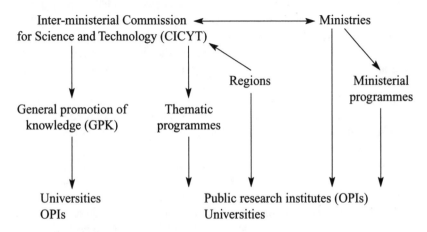

Figure 2.3   Social environmental research in Spain

The Spanish research system is obviously different from those in the richer countries, yet some variation between Spain and Greece can also be observed, see Figure 2.3. Spain accounts for 77 per cent in terms of territory and 60 per cent in terms of the total population of the EU's 'Objective 1 regions' in which the level of economic development is lower than the European average. By contrast with the Greek case, however, EU structural funds have not been used to fund environmental research. While European cohesion funds have been allocated for environmental activities, very few of these bear traces of social environmental approaches. As in Greece, capacity in social environmental research is low; unlike the situation in Greece, research is *not* strongly driven by ministries, even in public research institutes. This is probably due to the historically small role played by the state in relation to research, though, as we will see, the system has changed considerably in the past two decades.

It must be noted that the meaning of 'environment' in Spain is oriented towards agricultural development, thus carrying with it a necessarily regional focus. The notion of *global* environment has diffused into the general consciousness, but less so in research terms. Again, as in the case of Greece, this must be understood in relation to the gap in economic equity between southern and northern countries. On the other hand, research conducted under the national Energy Plan is much closer in content to other European research in this area; however, it is heavily oriented towards technological objectives and is, so far, lacking in social environmental explorations.

Until the end of the Franquist regime, the Spanish state's role in research was limited to funding a few minor public research centres through direct budgetary appropriations. Until 1986, almost no significant funding activity was developed using procedures in which investigators could obtain funds in a competitive framework. A number of structural changes set the stage for the rise of state-funded research, including accession to the European Community in 1986 and the change from a central to a quasi-federal state. Various legal reforms introduced in the 1980s were also responsible, expanding the function of universities from teaching to research, and clearing the way for the creation of a national R&D Plan. Applied research under this plan includes work on agriculture, environment and climate. Of the sectoral plans developed by various ministries, the Agrarian Plan and the Energy Plan are the most relevant in terms of environmental research.

State-funded research in universities is balanced by work in public research institutes which carry out the bulk of what little exists in Spain in terms of environmental and social environmental research. Of these, the Institute of Energy Studies has developed a programme on 'socioeconomic studies on energy and environment'. Irrespective of its location, Spanish research is not strongly linked to policy in any coordinated way. Thus regional ministries involved in developing environmental regulations appear to have little formal interaction with research. If the objectives listed in research project proposals are any indication, it appears that projects are only tenuously linked to perceived social problems.

As in most other countries, Finnish interest in the environment as a distinct policy area developed in the early 1980s. The Finnish Ministry of the Environment was founded in 1983, but it was not until 1993 that a National Commission on Sustainable Development was established with the aim of promoting cooperation between the government, private companies, NGOs and other interest groups. The commission's launching document called for research using a multidisciplinary approach. Environmental research has come to be viewed as a strategic tool of environmental policy making. It is in this context that the commission expects the social sciences to play a key role alongside the natural and technological sciences, see Figure 2.4.

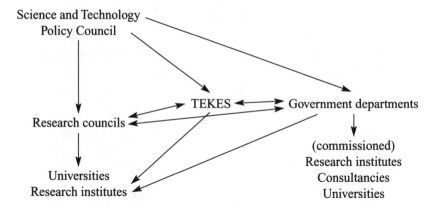

Figure 2.4   Social environmental research in Finland

In contrast to the government department-led systems in Austria and Greece, research is governed by the Academy of Finland. The Academy's four research councils cover the following areas: culture and society, natural sciences and engineering, health, and environment and natural resources. The councils interact closely with the Technology Development Centre (TEKES) which funds programmes on environmental and energy technologies, among other areas deemed relevant to industrial competitiveness. Research council members are chosen from the scientific community for three-year terms. Funding for social environmental research is principally through social science sub-areas in the Environment and Natural Resources Council which is generally dominated by the natural science disciplines. Hence, while the human dimensions of the environment are recognized, strong disciplinary support for social science approaches is missing.

Since the late 1980s, the Academy has also been establishing independent research programmes in fields that are developing fast, and those otherwise deemed to be of scientific and/or national importance. Developed and funded in conjunction with the Finnish Ministry of the Environment, two programmes on sustainable development and climate change are the most relevant for our purposes. They represent a partial move towards the institutionalization of social environmental research on a national basis.

Research on environmental problems, the impetus for which was similar to that in other countries, is highly developed in the Netherlands. Growth in environmental consciousness was prompted by international developments, most notably the report of the Brundtland Commission in 1987 and the first report of the Intergovernmental Panel on Climate Change (IPCC) in 1990. Social environmental research is also strong in terms of total staff capacity and the

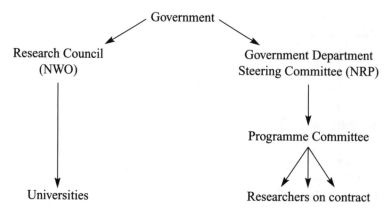

Figure 2.5   Social environmental research in the Netherlands

number of projects related to the field. At the same time, the research system is highly fragmented, with only a few topic areas having a critical mass of researchers, see Figure 2.5. We elaborate on this apparent paradox below.

The early 1990s were crucial for the development of social environmental research in the Netherlands. The Dutch Environmental Policy Plan of 1989 established a National Research Programme on Global Air Pollution and Climate Change, and called for the integration of research in this area with more emphasis on public policy over basic science. A 1990 report for the Ministry of Education and Science written by the then chairman of the Advisory Council for Environmental and Nature Research specifically stressed the need for programmes on social environmental research. A Dutch advisory committee on environmental economics provided further advice on ways of stimulating the development of environmental economics.

By the mid-1990s, several research programmes funded by ministries and other organizations were dedicated to social science work on the environment, and climate change in particular. In 1994, 260 of full-time staff equivalents in universities and 80 in other institutions could be classified as doing social environmental research. Thus, in terms of policy support, research capacity and international visibility, this field is well developed in the Netherlands. In the context of European environmental research, the country is in a uniquely strategic position, with both the researchers and the international networks to command influence disproportionate to its absolute size.

Yet these advantages have failed to lead to the consolidation of social environmental research in the form of well-resourced national programmes. The first reason for this is that 'social environmental' research exists as a secondary entity at the confluence of several discrete areas and without an identity of its own. Second, the very richness of resources and international networks available to researchers means that they are able to pursue their line of work *regardless* of the fragmented nature of social environmental research at the national level.

Likewise, the centrality of environmental policy in the Netherlands has actually helped dilute the research system dedicated to social environmental questions. The contours of the policy were established in the first National Environmental Plan of 1988/89. While environmental research was given a key role in environmental policy, the central research policy question was: 'how can research contribute to realizing a sustainable society in 2010?' Across the various funding bodies, research questions have, in turn, focused largely on implementation, appearing rather one-sided, technical or juridical in nature. However, there are signs that things might change. In 1997, the Dutch government responded to foresight initiatives with the proposal that social environmental research be better coordinated. The research council was also asked to assess the case for a centre devoted to social environmental research.

In any case, the question remains whether the very Europeanness of Dutch research and researchers has been at cross-purposes with the development of an integrated national research capacity. The international success of the leaders of the Dutch scientific community, playing prominent agenda-setting roles in the IPCC and the International Human Dimensions Programme (IHDP), seems to have been at a cost to the country's own research programme development.

The UK provides an interesting contrast to the Dutch case, see Figure 2.6. In 1988, in a speech to the Royal Society, then Prime Minister Margaret Thatcher called on scientists of all types to address the problems associated with climate change. This speech set the terms for much of the subsequent debate and contributed to the dramatic rise in funding for research – including social environmental research – on the global environment. Official documents

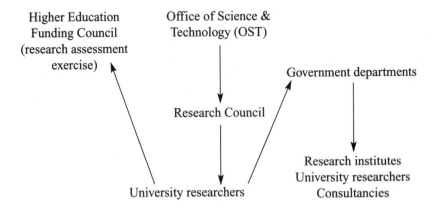

Figure 2.6   Social environmental research in the UK

and reports published throughout the 1990s have all signalled the objective of combining the benefits of a science-driven research effort with satisfying the demand for 'sustainable' growth.

The UK government's 1990 Environment White Paper, *This Common Inheritance*, laid out the following as key areas of concern: climate change, ozone depletion, acid rain, biodiversity losses, threats to food and water supply and quality, waste minimization, land use, energy policy and nuclear generation. While the contribution of the natural sciences was quickly recognized, the role of the social sciences was more contentious. In the 1980s, the emphasis had been on problems associated with 'scarcity' of resource supplies. In the 1990s, attention shifted towards the negative consequences, such as pollution and degradation of water and land resources, of 'plenty'. Research on the social impacts of environmental changes and on effective policy responses was still in its infancy, however. In most policy circles, environmental problems were treated as 'second order' problems that were neither as urgent nor as tractable as the problems of growth and development.

Blueprint for a Green Economy (Pearce *et al.*, 1989), the flagship document of the UK environmental economics community, paved the way to changing the view that environmental policy was harmful to economic development. An early version of this publication was produced for the UK Department of the Environment with part funding from the Economic and Social Research Council (ESRC). The importance of *Blueprint* was that it spoke to policy makers in a language they could easily understand, and served to convince them that policies such as fiscal reform and removal of energy subsidies could make a serious difference to environmental quality.

In early 1991, the ESRC launched the Global Environmental Change (GEC) Programme of research with a budget of over £20 million pounds and a lifetime of 10 years. Of the five national research councils, only the Natural Environment Research Council (NERC) had a programme budget of comparable size; in this context, it is worth emphasizing that the GEC programme was directed solely at social scientists. While the Department of the Environment continued to fund research by economists, the GEC Programme created an institutional core for social environmental research in the country.

The concentration of social environmental research capacity in one research programme has promoted a more competitive culture amongst social scientists and the universities themselves. At the time of the GEC Programme's third phase in 1994, nearly 400 research proposals had been submitted, but only about 30 funded, giving a 'strike rate' of one in 12. Competition has also been tight for environmental work carried out under the ESRC's open or so-called 'response mode' of research funding. This reflects the unusual size of the UK research community, especially in areas relevant to our case, such as development studies and environmental economics.

Like the other research councils in the UK, the ESRC is part of the Office for Science and Technology, which came to be transferred into the Department for Trade and Industry. A 1993 White Paper, *Realising our Potential*, issued on the heels of this shift, led the ESRC to redefine its mission around 'the needs of users and beneficiaries' with the expectation of 'contributing to the economic competitiveness of the United Kingdom ... and the quality of life'. In light of this, the GEC Programme began to put more emphasis on research addressing the role of business and industry in environmental issues.

The experience of the GEC Programme has been formative in a number of respects. It has influenced the evolution of Human Dimensions research in the EU's Fourth Framework Programme, as well as the development of other European environmental research programmes. The ESRC's involvement in bodies such as the International Group of Funding Agencies and the European Science Foundation, and the links developed by GEC researchers with their European counterparts have been instrumental in this regard.

The GEC Programme illustrates both the advantages and drawbacks of concentrating significant resources in a large, highly directed programme, linked to government objectives. On the one hand, it enabled social environmental researchers to make an impact on the general environmental agenda, quite out of proportion to the low level of funding they had traditionally enjoyed in relation to the natural sciences. By drawing in people from different disciplines, it also contributed to the creation of an 'internal market' of young researchers and to the creation of the field itself. On the other hand, the development of a policy-oriented programmatic agenda made it that much harder to preserve multiple perspectives (especially those from the more qualitative social sciences) within the field.

COMPARING NATIONAL RESEARCH SYSTEMS

The institutional framework of analysis outlined earlier in the chapter employed three main concepts: institutional structures, institutional rules (pragmatic and normative) and institutional change. In comparing national experiences of undertaking social environmental research, we can now operationalize this conceptual framework in terms of the following structural variables.

- *National research capacity* This variable translates the concept of an institutional structure to specific descriptions of types of organization in which research is carried out and their particular combination in different countries.
- *National programme development* This provides a further translation of the institutional structure concept.

- *National competition for research funding* This variable is a first-step specification of the idea of normative rules, that is, the broad limits and capacities for action prescribed by an institutional structure.
- *Degree of policy interaction* This variable is a second form by which normative rules may be specified.

Variations at these four levels across our six countries may then be used to explore the extent to which specifically national research agendas have developed, and their relationship to the European research agenda and practices. In turn, this interaction between national and European agendas provides an operationalization of our third analytic concept of institutional change.

The comparative analysis presented below draws from both the systemic overviews presented in the previous section and information from our database of European Union social environmental researchers. Using official data on projects funded by the Socio-Economic Environmental Research (SEER) and Human Dimensions of Environmental Change Programmes, we constructed a database of individual researchers who have been involved as coordinators or partners. These figures reflect a total of 558 such researchers from 25 countries.

National Research Capacity

Organizations funding social environmental research range from government departments, research councils and universities to non-governmental organizations (NGOs), corporations, consultancy companies and private research outfits. These organizations are combined in different ways in different research systems, hence generating country-specific institutional structures. Our aim is to try to explain the consequences of particular national configurations.

As suggested earlier, national research systems are themselves evolving within the broader framework of the European Union. So *to what extent are particular national institutional structures effective in managing demands from the wider research environment? What kinds of sub-structures and networks help manage the interfaces between national and European institutions?* To address these questions, let us first consider the organizational profile of social environmental researchers in different countries (Table 2.1). Except in the cases of Austria and Finland, individuals in the higher education (HE) sector generally outnumber their counterparts in all other organizations combined. In the UK, the country with the biggest number of researchers so far funded by EU social environmental research projects (89), 83 per cent (74) are based in the HE sector. On the other hand, Austria has 35 per cent (7) of its far smaller population of researchers based in universities; for Finland, the figure is 44 per cent (4). The high level of fragmentation of the Spanish research system is revealed by the distribution of researchers across all organizational sectors, though universities do still account for almost half (21 out of 43) of all EU-funded researchers. Finally, Greece has 76 per cent (19) and the Netherlands, 65 per cent (44) in the HE sector.

Table 2.1   Institutional profile of EU-funded social environmental researchers

	HES	RES	CONS	INDUS	GOVT	NGO	Other	Total
Austria	7	7	3	0	2	1	0	20
Finland	4	3	1	1	0	0	0	9
Greece	19	2	2	1	1	0	0	25
Netherlands	44	13	3	4	3	1	0	68
Spain	21	2	4	2	7	1	6	43
UK	74	7	3	1	3	1	0	89

Notes: Each row consists of the number of researchers (coordinators or partners in SEER and Human Dimensions projects) in each country, distributed by the type of organization in which they are based.

HES: higher education sector; RES: (private) research institute (not attached to university); CONS: private consultancy; INDUS: industrial enterprise; GOVT: government department/ laboratory (including parastatal organizations) NGO: non-governmental organisation.

Overall, we can say that institutional research capacity for social environmental research is low in Greece and Spain, given the extent of fragmentation in the form of lone researchers. In Austria and Finland, capacity in this area has taken off well. The Netherlands and the UK occupy the other end of the spectrum, with very high research capacity; however, the UK's research system is significantly more institutionalized on account of the high-profile Global Environmental Change Programme.

   The sheer size of the UK and Dutch contingents gives these two countries a relative advantage in terms of effective management of the national–European research interface. But more specifically, the existence of what may be called *serial research groups* (see Table 2.2) helps mediate between the two levels, creating an institutional sub-structure in the process. In Chapter 3, we elaborate on the notion of individual 'serial operators', that is, those researchers who consistently participate in SEER and Human Dimensions of Environmental Change projects, and are also active agenda setters in other international social environmental research initiatives. In our set of serial operators, we include all individuals who have been involved in three or more EU-funded projects. The parallel category of serial research groups refers to the organizational homes of these individuals (so long as they have continued to work in the same research centre or institute).

Table 2.2   Institutions involved in three or more SEER/Human Dimensions projects ('serial research groups')

Country	Department/Centre	Parent Institution
Austria	N/A	Institut fuer Oekologische Wirtschaftsforschung
Greece	Department of Sociology	University of Crete
Netherlands	Faculteit Bestuurskunde	University of Twente
Netherlands	Instituut voor Milieuvraagstukken	Vrije University, Amsterdam
Netherlands	Department of Leisure Studies	University of Tilburg
United Kingdom	Science Policy Research Unit (SPRU)	University of Sussex
United Kingdom	Centre for Social Economic Research on the Global Environment (CSERGE)	University of East Anglia and University College, London
United Kingdom	Centre for the Study of Environmental Change (CSEC)	University of Lancaster
United Kingdom	N/A	Institute for European Environmental Policy
United Kingdom	Centre for Environmental Technology	Imperial College

Concentration of social environmental work in the form of multiple projects enables serial research groups both to obtain funding resources, and, in turn, to use their reputation to act as national representatives in the European domain. Likewise, the visibility afforded by their high level of institutionalization means that EU research managers know where to turn for advice and support in setting the agenda for research. In this way, such a sub-structure can also help negotiate the interface between national and European levels. As Table 2.2 shows, Dutch and UK institutions dominate as European agenda setters and negotiators in this regard.

National Programme Development

The issue here is the institutionalization of research in the form of a national 'programme' of social environmental research, as opposed to a set of dispersed activities. Clearly, the concentration of research in this area under one umbrella reflects a particular type of organizational sub-structure. However, we can take one step backwards and ask whether the presence or absence of such programmes are themselves based on other institutional factors characterizing each national research system. Such a question could be contrasted with the more straightforward expectation that national social environmental research programmes simply reflect the rising salience of social issues related to the environmental agenda.

From the overviews of national systems presented above, we already know that the UK has a 10-year programme in this area. While the UK's is the most high-profile and the most concentrated, Austria, Finland and the Netherlands also have programmes in various stages of development. These take the form of multiple programmes devoted to certain generic environmental issues within which social environmental work is funded to varying degrees. By contrast, the UK's Global Environmental Change programme has originated from a rather more mixed range of influences.

Thus the rise of environmental consciousness and the growing salience of international issues – in particular, sustainable development and the broader problems of 'plenty' over the older resource scarcity paradigm – have been instrumental in programme development in all four countries. This has especially been the case in the Netherlands, a country that has taken the lead in environmental policy. However, in the UK, active lobbying by a select group of social scientists was also crucial in the setting up of a programme, the further development of which was shaped by the 'users and beneficiaries' focus of the 1993 White Paper, *Realising our Potential*. By contrast, in Austria, it is the central government that continues to exert a key influence, with the creation by one of its ministries of a national network for environmental research.

National Competition for Research Funding

This variable refers to what may be called the 'hunger' with which individuals pursue funding for research. As will be discussed in Chapter 3, individual researchers' need for funds helps explain both their involvement in European projects and their career trajectories. Since the 'hunger' for European funds is dependent on the scale of overall national research funding available relative to the size of the national research community, this variable may also reflect the extent to which a specifically 'national' social environmental research agenda has developed.

First, let us consider the level of competition for research funds in general in the six countries. Relative scarcity in research money available to all social scientists could well be a significant factor in stimulating the turn towards a new area (social environmental research) promoted by the European Union. Again, the UK stands out in terms of the extent to which researchers jostle for research funding. An extremely competitive environment is therefore part and parcel of the country's high research capacity that we previously outlined. Interestingly, such competition may be said to exist *owing to* the existence of a national programme devoted specifically to social environmental research, rather than *despite* it. While competition for social science funding is not so extreme in the Netherlands, there are definite similarities with the UK scenario. In Finland, by contrast, there is a relatively high level of support for social science work on technology issues, so that researchers are not equally attracted by social environmental research money simply on account of a generic 'hunger' for funds. However, there is relatively high competition for national social environmental research funding on its own terms. While Austria, Greece and Spain are very different in terms of the small size of the research force and amount of funding, they share an academic environment in which levels of competition are low. On the other hand, the perceived *adequacy* of national funds that do exist for research is much higher in Austria than in their Mediterranean counterparts.

Degree of Policy Interaction

The variable in this case is the extent to which research has been geared towards policy impacts, usually in the hands of governments or other bodies wishing to shape the research agenda. The relevant contrast here is to so-called 'responsive' research which is largely formulated by the research community itself to meet intellectual or academic goals. In practice, little social science research on the environment is merely responsive: it is usually put forward with some attention to emerging political and policy issues.

While university work funded by research councils may also be geared towards policy and greater interaction with potential 'users', it can still be distinguished in terms of degree of policy interaction from research that is formally commissioned by non-academic bodies. Governmental researchers are likely to be in closer day-to-day contact with policy officials, often being so much part of policy-making circles that they make the research–policy distinction irrelevant in this regard. Thus we can return to our figures on the institutional profile of social environmental research in different countries (Table 2.1) and draw some qualified conclusions about the extent to which research is conducted in close interaction with either government policy or the requirements of private bodies or NGOs.

Although, as we have pointed out, a system of government-led research has been the norm in countries like Austria and Greece, the number of social environmental researchers funded directly by government bodies is nevertheless small (two out of 20, and one out of 25 researchers, respectively). The small percentage of such funding is the norm in the other countries as well. This, as our interviews suggest, is because social environmental expertise has not yet been widely seen as relevant for practical, day-to-day government problems. On the other hand, social environmental research in the Netherlands is strikingly directed towards policy implementation, despite the fact that very few

Table 2.3   Comparison of national social environmental research systems

Country	Research capacity	Programme development	Competition for funding	Interaction with policy
Austria	Based in universities, research institutes	Ministry-funded network, SUSTAIN	Funding from ministries; perception of adequate funds	Formal networks linking researchers and ministries due to funding patterns
Finland	Based in universities	Research academy programmes (sustainability and climate change)	Well-funded system for technology-related social research; fairly high competition for social environmental research funds	Some applied research for ministries
Greece	Few individuals scattered across universities	No programme	Limited nationally funded research; limited competition	Limited research for government; mostly data collection
Netherlands	Large number of university researchers, but low critical mass in most areas	Multiple programmes Prospect of social environmental research centre being assessed	Competition for funding from multiple sources	Close interaction between ministries and research
Spain	Few individuals scattered across universities, public research institutes	No programme	Limited nationally funded research; limited competition	Little emphasis on research for policy
UK	Large number of university researchers, concentrated in research groups	High-profile research council-funded GEC programme on social environmental research	University budget constraints; high competition for external funds	Increasing pressure for policy relevance from research council

researchers are directly funded within government (three out of 68). Finally, it is worth emphasizing that research may sometimes be influential on policy in terms of bringing in new ideas and approaches (such as the social sciences into the environment) when it arrives in the shape of an outsider. In other words, day-to-day interaction between research and government clearly does make for influence, but only of a certain kind.

Table 2.3 summarizes the major points of our comparative analysis of the six different national systems in Europe we studied.

THE DEVELOPMENT OF NATIONAL RESEARCH AGENDAS

Stepping back from the four institutional variables in national research systems discussed above, we can now ask how they contribute to the development of, particularly, national research agendas in social environmental research – if, indeed, such definable agendas do exist. Secondly, we can explore their interaction with European research agendas, in particular the extent to which one level has been able to exert a significant 'steering' influence on the other. How do institutional structures change to accommodate new areas of research and new research agendas? This question will be pursued in the rest of this chapter.

What is particularly interesting in our research findings is that, despite significant national differences in levels of research capacity, structures of competition for funds and institutional research structures in general, there is relatively little in the various social environmental research agendas that has a distinctively national stamp. The exception, in this regard, is perhaps the Netherlands, where, as we have pointed out, a strong orientation exists towards supplying research for policy implementation. However, this is an emergent agenda for research that is an artefact of the fragmented nature of the Dutch institutional system. Ironically, multiple programmes spread across various research centres enable the creation of a common mind-set insofar as environmental policy is perceived in piecemeal fashion to refer to discrete issues such as water quality, air pollution or land use.

If the Dutch system is one example of a latent research agenda created out of a diffuse system, we could equally turn to the other end and point out that Spain, too, exhibits fragmentation, albeit of a very different sort. Rather than multiple research centres together pursuing many social environmental research projects, we have a system of lone researchers scattered across Spanish universities with very few projects between them. Yet Spain, along with Greece, has been able to raise questions about equity in the gaps that continue to exist in the European agenda for ecological modernization (see Chapter 4). This brings us to the broader question of the extent to which the national and the European do influence each other.

In some cases the European research agenda is almost the same as that for an individual country; in other cases it is distinct. In some cases the European agenda has actively helped shape the national research; in other cases the national research has materially contributed to the development of the European agenda. This wider issue of the links between national and European levels of research activity is discussed in Chapters 5 and 6, but is referred to here as another example of the comparative framework we are seeking to develop. Two themes emerge from this comparison. The first concerns the flow of research questions between national and European levels. It is clear that the UK and the Netherlands have been very influential in shaping the European agenda, moving their own research priorities onto the European list. On the other hand, Greece and Spain appear to define their own national research priorities largely through reference to the European agenda. Finland and Austria do have their own priorities which they attempt to foster and seek to exploit at the European level.

The second theme concerns perceptions of useful research. Our national studies suggest that there are huge variations in policy makers' experience of social science research and, consequently, their expectations of what constitutes a relevant role: data collection, data analysis, critical analysis of policy and so on. EU research funding has had a marked effect on these perceptions of policy usefulness at the different national levels where the very nature of 'research activity' is being subjected to redefinition. From the standpoint of the EU, in the meanwhile, arguments for engaging different researchers in European-level research are complex, and include both the need to harness existing research capacity (UK, Dutch) and develop latent capacity in other countries (Spain, Greece).

Returning to the institutional framework of analysis introduced in the first part of this chapter, we can now pose this question: given the big differences in level of research competition (variable 2), and in research capacity (variable 1) in the six countries we have studied, to what extent is there agreement about the rules which govern competition, and a clear understanding of how to 'play the game'? With its focus on individual researcher behaviour and the pragmatic rules governing it, the next chapter attempts to address this question.

3. New researchers, new institutions

INTRODUCTION

The dynamics of research depend, in any model, on individuals. They are the ones who bring ideas into research programmes, set up joint partnerships with others like themselves, participate in meetings and move from one initiative or project to another. Within the framework of institutional structures and normative rules outlined in the previous chapter, a set of *pragmatic rules* for action evolves as researchers go about the business of setting up and carrying out research. This chapter therefore turns towards an individual perspective on the dynamics of European social environmental research.

Chapter 2 elaborated upon key elements of the national context within which European research is organized, promoted, practised and perceived, and provided a hint of the interrelationships between national and European levels. Individual researchers are the carriers who populate and move between these two macro levels; a focus on the micro level is therefore the obvious next step. A micro perspective implies, on the one hand, exploring the ways in which individuals have shaped and been shaped by different institutional structures and normative rules, and, on the other, tracing the consequences of such structures and rules for their own behaviour and career trajectories. Recent developments in global environmental policy and European research policy (outlined in Chapter 1) set the background against which researchers have come to participate in and create a new field of enquiry. In the course of their participation, they, in turn, have influenced the dynamics and institutional development of social environmental research in their own countries and at the European level.

Even a cursory look at our EU database of social environmental researchers is sufficient to note that, quite apart from national variation, the individuals involved have very different intellectual histories. Given that social environmental research as it is constituted today is a field that emerged only in the 1990s, we would like to establish how, and why, people from different disciplines and research backgrounds came to be involved in this enterprise. Do they constitute a coherent *epistemic community*, that is, a group of influential experts with shared knowledge relating to a specific policy-making domain (Haas, 1992)? The variety of answers that researchers provide regarding their *rationale for involvement* in national and European social environmental research systems helps shed light on this question. Rationales cited include such factors as a vocational or political commitment to the environment, the 'hunger for funds' in particular national systems, otherwise unavailable intellectual opportunities, and the prestige and reputational spin-offs bestowed upon careers. Exploring this complex web of individual motivations is also useful for exploring the broad structure of *incentives and barriers* to entry that are perceived to exist in this field of research. We focus on these issues shortly.

Since international collaboration is a defining feature of EU-supported research activity, we want also to provide insights into the realities of *'project making'*, that is, the practices and strategies involved in establishing and working with an international team of researchers. The chapter moves on to take up this aspect, complementing the picture of multiple individual motivations for European involvement with one of shared incentives and obstacles for cross-national collaboration. On the one hand, this analysis reveals the importance of individual reputations as well as of prior personal contacts and networks in bringing a core group of people together. On the other hand, what may be seen as 'shotgun weddings' also appear to be common practice, engendered partly by EU hopes for promoting Europe-wide cohesion via collaboration between southern and northern countries. We also devote attention to the special role played by project coordinators in shaping both the content of the proposal and the rules of the 'game' – that is, the day-to-day interactions and negotiations between project partners – that is to be embarked upon.

Turning from individual projects to the research portfolio that some individuals manage to accumulate, we examine the development of *career trajectories* within European social environmental research. The making of reputations is of crucial interest here. We contrast the experience of serial operators with that of research assistants in the evolution of individual reputations and careers. In Chapter 2, we referred to serial research groups as those centres and institutes with a track record of participation in multiple European projects, as well as in other international programmes and initiatives. Serial operators are those well-connected, frequently sought-after individuals located in such centres. Their names tend to crop up, not just as coordinators or partners in more than a few projects, but also in consultative workshops and committees involved in making policy for social environmental research. On the other hand, research assistants and junior researchers tend to lead a more fragmented existence, balancing the need to make a living and/or find a PhD topic against the insecurities of being involved in an emerging, interdisciplinary field with uncertain career prospects for the future. In either case, European social environmental research can be seen as a field of action which both shapes and is shaped by the trajectories of individual researchers.

In the concluding section of this chapter we reflect on the structure of the social order that emerges as individuals navigate and, in the process, create the social environmental research system.

CONVENTIONS AND CURRENCIES OF EXCHANGE IN EPISTEMIC COMMUNITIES: A FRAMEWORK FOR ANALYSIS

This chapter has a micro-level focus in that it relates the experiences and perceptions recounted by individual researchers. However, we frame these individual narratives within the context of an analytical perspective that is no less institutionalist than the one employed in our survey of national research systems. Located in the sociology of science (Barnes and Edge, 1982), this framework focuses on the social conventions and currencies of exchange that structure the activities of any research community and influence the knowledge they produce as well as its transmission (Shove, 2000). In the sociological tradition, institutions are, in effect, those conventions that take on a 'rule-like' status in social action (DiMaggio and Powell, 1991, p. 9). Whether conventions are the emergent aggregate of individual actions or prior structures that shape these actions is a debate that we will refrain from entering into in this context. Rather, in line with structuration theory, we simply note that the individual and the institutional constitute each other.

The Mertonian tradition in the sociology of knowledge argued that science was organized in such a way that its system for exchanging and communicating information was simultaneously also a system for allocating individual rewards (Merton, 1973; see also Barnes and Edge, 1982). The journal publication was, of course, the jewel in the crown of the scientific system. Scientists would offer up their research results as veritable 'gifts' (Hagstrom, 1965) to a community of peers for judgment of their worth; in the absence of monetary exchange, the symbolic recognition afforded by publication was the scientist's reward. As the rise of research funded by so-called 'soft money' became ever more evident, scholars began to challenge this notion of science as a system governed by a set of rules different from that of ordinary economic markets. Scientists came to be seen as continually engaged in the act of converting one form of 'capital' to another, thereby working their way through what might be seen as a *cycle of credibility* (Latour and Woolgar, 1979). Rather than being a reward in itself, credibility is a form of 'credit' which allows a variety of moves: for example, recognition created by a recent publication adds to a scientist's stock of credibility, which can then be cashed in as a research grant, which, in turn, enables investment in new resources (equipment, people and so on) for the generation of new research; and so on.

In recent years, this exchange/conversion model of scientific activity has come to be applied to the study of social science communities particularly in the context of new trends in the organization of university research (Gibbons *et al.*, 1994). A key issue here is how researchers, their activities and conventions have been influenced by the emergent multiplication of knowledge producers and users. These have generated competing pressures and divergent expectations that spill well beyond the scientific community. As the role of knowledge claims in policy domains becomes relevant, the term 'epistemic community' as defined by Haas (1992) captures the nature of such hybrid groups better than the more traditionally academic 'scientific community'. An epistemic community may be defined as 'a network of professionals with recognised expertise and competence in a particular domain and an authoritative claim to policy-relevant knowledge within that domain or issue-area' (ibid., p. 3). Such a community typically consists of not only academics or scientists, but also other professionals, including research policy managers and policy makers. Especially in the environmental field, such communities operate through and between international as well as national networks.

Social researchers develop and display multiple identities in the course of their respective careers as they struggle to create and maintain positions for themselves across the range of user and academic networks inhabited by an epistemic community. The notion of multiple identities goes beyond the mere fact that researchers typically have two-way contacts with other scientists, policy makers and the public at large. It means also that researchers have become entrepreneurs, strategically managing their 'merchandise' and devising new ways of producing, marketing and selling it. In the course of their day-to-day work, they operate in several 'research regimes' rather than a single, unified research system. Thus they face and respond differently to different sets of incentives and conventions (Shove, 2000).

In the arena of European research, individual reputation or credibility is created and managed through the negotiation of perceptions as well as the formal products of reports and publications. Quid pro quo exchanges between researchers, and between researchers and policy managers, include money, in the form of research contracts or awards, but also time, effort and attention devoted to each other. Through these reciprocal interactions, the researcher becomes known. Reputation is crucial, not only for researchers in identifying potential collaborators, but also for research managers in making decisions about reliable research providers in distributing funds. Thus individual reputation has an institutionally important role, in that it is bound up in various reciprocal relationships and overlapping networks. In turn, researchers spend a fair amount of their working time 'networking', since being well-connected is fundamental to getting a foot in different fields of action and, once in, becoming attuned to different conventions in order to maintain and expand their level of involvement. The role of networking is all the more important since the system of EU funding is designed to be equitable, open and transparent. In other words, convergence and density around 'key' individuals seems to be the product of institutional dynamics rather than of intentional bias or nepotism.

In the following sections we examine the lives of European social environmental researchers and projects in the context of the framework outlined above. Thus the influence of serial operators can be understood in terms of the density of their social networks rather than the content of their research products per se. More generally, the building up of individual reputations and the creation of an elite cadre of researchers are both outcomes of a complex set of reciprocal interactions between people, and the exchange of money and contacts as well as ideas. In this regard, European social environmental research cannot be seen solely as an *epistemic* community as defined by Haas, since it is not just knowledge that is the relevant unit of production and exchange. In turn, the multiple currencies structuring research activity and the stratification between elite and other researchers mean that the community itself cannot be seen as a homogeneous one. Finally, by examining the making of social environmental research projects in terms of our exchange model, we also find that the research agenda, rather than simply being imposed by national and European systems, is actively negotiated, produced and transformed through the course of multiple interactions between researchers and research managers.

INCENTIVES AND BARRIERS TO EUROPEAN INVOLVEMENT

The first question that must necessarily be posed about individual involvement is whether there is such a thing as an identifiable community in European social environmental research. While this section will go on to show that multiple motivations are at play and that forms of involvement vary, we can start by asking whether researchers perceive themselves to be part of such a coherent group, or might different individuals identify with different levels – national, regional or disciplinary – within the extended research network? This question may be fruitfully addressed by returning to one of the key variables explored in Chapter 2, namely the level of institutionalization of social environmental research within different countries.

We have seen that the extent to which social environmental research is institutionalized varies enormously, being highest in the UK and the Netherlands, and lowest in Greece and Spain. Individuals in countries with formal research programmes and networks (such as SUSTAIN and OIN in Austria, and the GEC Programme in the UK) have an opportunity to identify themselves as part of a 'social environmental research community' in its own right. In these cases, a set of communal relationships between individual researchers is, in effect, structured by a 'top-down' process.

By contrast, Spanish researchers do not share a similar sense of community that is specifically social environmental in nature. They mostly claim adherence to a traditional academic discipline such as agricultural economics or institutional economics. Others with long experience in a relatively new sub-field claim allegiance to a community of 'environmental economics' or 'ecological economics' rather than to 'social environmental research'. This brings us back to the fact that, in Spain, as in Greece, the field consists of individuals scattered across various organizations, each of whom happen to have worked on one or more projects that may be said to fit the social environmental label. These individuals may know each other because of informal contacts, but this does not give them the feeling of working under a common institutional or intellectual umbrella. Insofar as they exist, networks emerge in 'bottom-up' fashion, rather than on account of strategic promotion by the state or national research council.

Yet we must guard against exaggerating the whole idea of individuals in coherent communities even in countries that have well-structured national programmes. If, as we do in this chapter, we conceive of researchers as individuals who develop multiple identities throughout their careers, the idea that they are simultaneously part of *different* communities becomes more plausible. This point was raised in one of our interviews by a UK researcher ('Sam') who identified three different types of community: disciplinary, interdisciplinary and policy, the last of which involves government officials as well as academics. Once this diversity has been recognized, we can situate the various communities and individual identities within a system of two interlocking research regimes, one national, the other European.

Institutional Context

The institutional stimulus for researcher involvement in social environmental research may take different shapes. This may range from the promise of higher status from participation in a prestigious international network to rather more mundane monetary reasons. Especially relevant are those reasons that create a *hunger for funds*, thereby driving individuals to extend their search for financial support. We have already noted in Chapter 2 that the UK has an extremely competitive research environment, with strong pressures in universities for academics to search for external funds. Our interviews suggest that the hunger for funds seems to be the most extreme in the UK in relation to other European countries. Yet even in countries like Spain a few research institutions do experience a similar demand for funds.

BOX 3.1

'Steve' (UK) works at a research centre with financial problems which have since been surmounted by participation in EU work, amongst other external projects. He notes: 'We were doing a lot of research council projects which did not generate very much overheads. So one bit of advice from our centre was to do some EU consulting.'

BOX 3.2

'Maria' (Spain) is a biologist at a research centre formerly funded by the Ministry of Industry and Energy. Severe cuts in public funds have pushed researchers to find external sources of financing. Maria has responded to these pressures by getting involved in several EU projects, as well as research networks.

The case of 'Maria' reminds us that institutional hunger for funds is unlikely to be satisfied by one-off involvement in a single project. The promise of future involvement in new projects may serve as further motivation for individuals to get a foot in the door. The expectation of spin-offs for the future could revolve around new EU projects, or participation in other international projects and forums. In this context, the 'social relations' or networking prospects associated with European work may be at least as attractive as the content of the research itself. Individuals will rarely espouse such opportunistic motivations outright, by contrast with the more socially acceptable moral, or intellectual commitments that we explore next. However, 'Gary', a UK researcher, was refreshingly open in this regard. He admitted to taking up a highway consultancy's invitation to conduct a social impact assessment, despite not already knowing much about the subject or the road scheme, because as head of his department 'he wasn't going to turn down the chance of money'. Yet, insofar as individual 'hunger for funds' is part of a 'hungry' institutional structure, a certain degree of opportunism is perhaps inevitably present in the strategies of many social environmental researchers.

On the other hand, in some cases, the institution may create *dis*incentives for the researcher to become more involved in European research. This is especially true for Spanish researchers holding a permanent academic position which does not depend on their carrying out research, though they may want to do so to satisfy their intellectual curiosity. In Greek and Spanish universities, the general rule is that obtaining external funds does not directly translate into higher remuneration or prestige. This is partly because, as we have already mentioned, research networks within these countries exist only in a loose sense, and there is little sense of a national community that might bestow recognition and honours. The combination of university funding structures and a system revolving around leading professors and their teams of students means that research entrepreneurs are relatively uncommon.

In contrast with what happens in universities, the situation of social environmental researchers in private public foundations and in some public research institutions seems to operate as expected: that is, the more one publishes and rises in reputation, the higher the rank/status and salary accorded. However, this too varies across research centres, even in the same country. For instance, it is generally true for CIEMAT (Spain) where institutional hunger for funds is high, but does not hold in the case of CSIC (*Consejo Superior de Investigaciones Científicas*, also in Spain) where such 'hunger' on the part of both the institution and researchers holding a permanent position is limited.

Finally, in southern countries with limited administrative capacity for handling externally funded projects, some researchers are discouraged from European involvement by the bureaucratic requirements. For example, researcher 'Manuel' (Spain), decided to restrict project applications to the minimum, since he felt that the time investment is a sunk cost which cannot be recovered in the event of failure to secure funding. For 'Carlos' (Spain), 'bureaucratic problems related to the lack of knowledge, on the part of researchers, of how to fill papers for EU projects, and the lack of specialized personnel in the administrative services of universities is one of the reasons why there are so few Spanish researchers coordinating EU projects'.

Vocational Commitment

The central tenet of this section (and indeed of the chapter) is that, from the individual perspective, institutions matter. Institutions create incentives and barriers that influence the behaviour of researchers, yet they do not completely determine individual actions. The behaviour and strategies adopted by social environmental researchers emerge from a more complex negotiation of personal motivations and institutional structures.

Ranking high among such individual motivations for some researchers is a personal commitment to environmental issues. Such commitment could be manifested in terms of prior political involvement in environmental movements and/or a vocational interest in 'the environment' as *the* major moral issue of the day. The vocational factor seems to be especially relevant in the case of Spanish researchers, amongst whom hunger for funds is relatively low when compared with other European researchers. For example, an economist, 'Juan' (Spain), reckons that he had multiple motivations for engaging in social environmental research, but 'in the final analysis moral–ethical motivations were the most important ones'.

BOX 3.3

'Terttu' is a senior Finnish researcher. He traces his research interest to his involvement in the environmental movement on account of river-water quality problems in his home town. While he would prefer to be a professor, no professorship exists for this sub-discipline at his university. In any case, he seems to be genuinely motivated by his 'cause', in that he has not made special efforts to gear his work towards money or position.

On the other hand, activist involvement in environmental movements or NGOs seems to be shared by a number of senior researchers in Northern and Central European countries. In this case, individual research agendas were influenced by the rise of an environmental movement and the first international environmental conferences held in the 1970s.

Intellectual Challenge

Alternatively, some researchers may be interested in social environmental research primarily because of the intellectual challenges posed to their discipline. For example, one agricultural economist decided to work on ecological economics in the belief that economics needed to broaden its perspectives by taking environmental, sociological and political analysis into account. Likewise, another Spanish researcher noted that, since funding opportunities were already abundant in his country, 'the possibility of solving an interesting problem and the prospect of personally enjoying the theme of research' constituted the real spur to his involvement in social environmental work.

The chance to carry out research of an *interdisciplinary* nature as generally promoted by the EU is an especially important intellectual attraction. One of our interviewees, 'Alan' (UK) viewed interdisciplinary work 'as a way of injecting fresh air in the discipline, of coming out of the margins. They are the kind of projects that are going in the interstices of things. Debate in the discipline needs to be thrashed out.' Certainly, in some countries research of this character is currently being funded by national sources, but others need to turn to the European level for similar opportunities.

BOX 3.4

'Rob' (UK) reports, 'If you're going to bring in modern methodology, you need to be rooted in your discipline, and come together because you have a common interest. Having this opportunity from DG XII validates work that people are doing as important; it allows room for softer work on the environment rather than something which is purely economic modelling, as something to which economists have an important contribution to make.'

In addition, EU projects offer the chance to carry out *comparative* research. For some of the people we interviewed, this aspect was something they specifically valued in submitting proposals for an EU-funded project. For example, 'Fred' (UK) was keen on doing comparative work, but needed to do so collaboratively in order to surmount the foreign language problem that would inevitably pose problems for the acquisition of cross-national data. Also another claimed characteristic of EU research, one particularly surprising for UK researchers when compared to their research council sources, is the theoretical nature of work being funded. 'Jack' (UK) observes that, 'in retrospect, it is astounding that DGXII paid for such a theoretical piece of work. When you put something in to ESRC it may be very theoretical but you play down this part and put more in about what you're actually going to do.'

On the other hand, the division of labour within the social sciences and between the natural and social sciences puts intellectual hurdles in the path to European social environmental research. Where such research is less institutionalized, this may lead to individuals falling back on the familiar certainties of research assessment criteria structured in terms of disciplinary preoccupations. Yet, even in countries like the UK with a strong professional network in social environmental research, junior researchers must negotiate the tensions involved in becoming attached to a field with an uncertain long-term future. Even some of those actually doing such work, albeit from within one of the disciplines, consider that 'knowledge only advances through specialization' and reckon that interdisciplinary research is, more or less, marginal.

Finally, it must be noted that research centres that appear to carry the mantle of 'interdisciplinary research' with pride may just be encouraging research in different disciplines with little intellectual connection between projects. For example, 'Liz' (UK) describes the centre in which she works as 'very inter-disciplinary in terms of individual backgrounds, but not necessarily in terms of project work as everyone works in isolation up to a point'. Even in the case of interdisciplinary research being funded by the EU, the integration of disciplines seems to be more a desired objective than a reality.

Disciplinary Commitment

For economists, 'personal commitment' is less likely to be movement-related or based on generic social responsibility and more likely to be based on a pro-fessional responsibility to assist in policy making. For example, 'Sam' (UK) sees himself as an economist mainly concerned with how his discipline can help improve policy debate. He therefore adapted his prior intellectual interest in fiscal policy to work on the subject of environmental taxes. Sociologists, geographers and political scientists seem more likely to cite an interest in a social movement which, over time, became transformed into an intellectual interest. An example here is 'Michel' (UK), an established researcher in political science, whose initiation into environmental issues came through his involvement in the French anti-nuclear movement and in red–green coalitions in Britain. However, he went on to develop an interest in intellectual perspec-tives from social theory, which he now seeks to 'marry' to those in environmental activism. Or consider 'Fred' (UK), who has successfully integrated intellectual concerns in the sociology of science with a personal interest in the environment derived from a reading of Schumacher in the 1970s and from his then wife who was doing research on environmental groups.

Vocational commitment to the environment and to social environmental work may also come from the fact that some researchers' intellectual training already seems closely linked to environmental issues. Social environmental research, in this context, may seem like a natural extension of their discipline, rather than a challenge to it (as with the mainstream social sciences). In Spain, this is especially the case with agricultural economists and agricultural engineers. In the UK and Finland, those working on energy issues likewise find it natural to move to the 'environment'.

New Opportunities

As an emerging interdisciplinary and policy-guided field, the SEER programme and its successor have created a new space for research, and subsequent oppor-tunities for networking and funding. We have already noted that the very existence of these opportunities may trigger involvement not necessarily based on a special interest in the substantive content of environmental research. One might say that, to some extent, demand creates supply. This process is tied to the creation and diffusion of the perception, especially strong in countries like the UK with a good infrastructure in this field, that social environmental research is a 'booming' area with excellent prospects for the future. People seem to feel that they 'have caught the right train'. In terms of our exchange model of research activity, such a field is ideal for multiple conversions by individuals of one form of capital to another; that is, one funding grant leads to another, which adds to the reputation and credibility of an individual, in turn leading to further success with new research proposals, and so on.

There is a general belief, expressed by 'Manuel' (Spain) for example, that rising environmental consciousness will increasingly push decision makers to collect data about socioeconomic processes in relation to the environment, superseding established, but rather technocratic, approaches. This will be an international process, given that international conferences and conventions are already the norm in the environmental arena. Belief in the 'boom' is leading to interesting strategic positioning by some researchers who have never been involved in environmental work.

For example, 'Steve' (UK) noted that he could not get funding for work characterized in terms of his primary interest in debates about urban technologies. Vested with an environmental flavour, however, his agenda succeeded in obtaining funds from the ESRC's Global Environmental Change Programme. As he sees it, 'what the environment has done quite clearly is to create space for new people, building a research agenda in response to the ESRC–GEC attempt to create a research agenda'. 'John' (UK) thinks that his move away from traditional philosophy to environment philosophy is part of a strategy in which he sees himself as 'slightly chameleon for different things in different worlds, as I became dissatisfied with a solitary world'. In any case, by cultivating a sub-disciplinary interest in the subject, such individuals may end up with a portfolio of work in which social environmental research is a prominent part, thereby providing them with a currency for future use.

Trade-offs between Incentives and Barriers

So far, we have referred to European funding opportunities in homogeneous terms, but researchers' perceptions on the value of engaging in European social environmental research depend, not just on the sheer amount of money available, but also on trade-offs between nationally funded and European projects. Country-level and EU research regimes carry different benefits and costs that researchers must work out and work within.

Thus, for example, UK researchers consider that, in purely financial terms, ESRC money is more beneficial. However, this needs to be traded off against the international prestige associated with European involvement. 'Liz' (UK) reckons that 'prestige is attached to EU money because it is hard to get and the research centre itself is run on project awards, and therefore you are only as good as the money you bring in'. But EU projects are also attractive for the opportunity they afford to do interdisciplinary work, when compared with the disciplinary based evaluation culture of ESRC peer review. One researcher, 'Jane' (UK), also remarked that the research she is interested in would not be funded by the ESRC because 'it disregards things that are just starting out, i.e., pump priming. The ESRC agenda is too narrow.'

The Dutch researchers we interviewed were interested in the funding opportunities that EU projects provide, while Spanish and Greek academics stressed the prestige from scientific output (publications) and new international contacts. This is related to 'civil servant syndrome', while the attitude of 'Maria', who works at a Spanish project-funded research centre, is closer to that of her UK peers.

BOX 3.5

'Rob' (UK) observes: 'Financially there is a very low margin in EU projects, so they are not important to the department in that sense – rather in terms of the extent to which they can lead to other things. For example, consultancy at the EU level, where there is a much higher margin and they are important for credibility. There is also internal advantage – to demonstrate within the university that one has done a lot of work at European level.'

As we mentioned before, future spin-offs from present EU projects are a reasonable expectation; thus the potential *indirect* financial benefits can also make involvement attractive. Opportunities for relatively profitable consultancy work at EU level could be enhanced by working on an EU project. In addition to this, these projects improve the image of the institution, which, in turn, may have positive financial consequences in the future.

Finally, the comparatively longer duration of European projects allows the creation of better opportunities for training and for setting up longer-term positions in research centres for junior researchers. This helps stimulate the development of research careers and, hence, research capacity for the future of the social environmental field. This issue was raised by some of the Spanish and UK researchers we interviewed.

So far in this chapter we have surveyed the variety of motivations that bring individuals to European social environmental research projects, but how do these projects themselves get set up? Since collaboration is a prerequisite for EU support, how do international partnerships of researchers actually work? It is to these questions that we now turn.

MAKING PARTNERSHIPS AND PROJECTS

In this section, we describe the conventions, practices and shared motivations that constitute the making of an EU project. Although drawn from the specific field of research we studied, our observations may bear some similarities to the development of projects in other domains. In this respect, the process of project making is likely to be influenced more by general features of the EU research landscape than by the content of the research area. Framed by the needs and goals of the EU's work programme, a project in social environmental research may take a number of forms.

- *A follow-up project* A research topic on which work was done in previous projects might need further research because of its long-term perspective and/or complexity.
- *The aggregation of knowledge and interests* Researchers realize, through dialogue with other researchers with whom they have informal contacts, that there is a general interest on the part of funders and potential gatekeepers in a certain project idea.
- *A partnership by coincidence* An individual has an idea for a project and needs a partner with a specific expertise or a better-known person as coordinator. Developing the project further may then be akin to a 'shotgun wedding' in which unknown collaborators are enlisted during a process of frantic phone calling as the deadline for application approaches.

The process of establishing the 'project group' in the cases we studied operates on fairly similar lines. Whatever the history of the research question or theme, it is typical for a core of researchers consisting of the coordinator and one or two 'qualified' partners to submit proposals for funding. These individuals may be part of the same formal or informal networks, or implicit ones, as in cases where researchers do not know each other personally but know each other's work. We found many instances in which one member of the core was a 'big node', that is, one who is well connected in the field and with a high reputation. Core members may know other people whom they consider interesting or relevant for the project for various reasons. In any case, it is their job to put together the team of partners and make the submission.

The shared motivations of this core group of people may be similar to the individual ones already described: the chance to undertake interdisciplinary research not supported by national sources, the capacity to overcome practically hurdles to obtaining reliable cross-country data, and so on. The project core acts strategically and looks for specific features in the other partners to be involved. When the theme is especially innovative or risky, the best known and established researchers may not necessarily be the most attractive and, indeed, could be perceived as a disadvantage. 'Steve' (UK) notes that his core group's agenda was an unusual one, and that 'when we met more established researchers who were doing work in this area they were too tightly framed. The way that they viewed the research world wasn't going to create space for us. We had to find other unusual types.'

The role of the coordinator is to draw up the 'rules of the game' which tend to conform to his or her own research interests or strategic position. Sometimes this may require providing the research partners with a certain flexibility. 'Steve' (UK) reports that he wrote the proposal and sent it to partners previously contacted for comments, 'specifying that the work should be empirical, regional and historical. I don't care what else, as long as the central theme is X.' Some researchers describe decisions about the role of different disciplines in the project and other methodological as well as conceptual issues as a negotiating procedure between actors with unequal 'power'. For 'Sarah' (UK), 'people are bringing their own disciplines to the project in ways that are unfolding and some become dominant depending on how forceful they are'.

How and why certain researchers are perceived by the core to be worthy of being invited to join the team is the next question. Usually, researchers get to know about each other through a chain of contacts: someone knows someone who knows someone, and so on. For example, 'Jack' (UK) observes that 'Robin never would have rung me up if he hadn't known me through Stephen and John, and they never would have known about me if it wasn't for my connection with Juergen.' The reasons for an individual being contacted are various.

- *Intellectual reputation*   There are those contacted for their intellectual capacity or past work done on similar or related issues. Credibility and reputation play an important role in this context. For 'Rob' (UK), 'the project is about choosing your friends from people you want to be associated with. It is about selecting partners who are at least the same academic standing as yourself, but it is not about reciprocal engagement. You're really looking for someone better than yourself to be engaged with which helps future credibility, to be seen to be in there with the right people.' On the other hand, Rob's project was successful in getting funds partly because of a rise in his own environmental profile from an ESRC grant.

- *Reputation for being networked* Some researchers are known to have a network of possible contacts. This is an asset from the coordinator's perspective because this researcher may know other interesting researchers who could be roped into the project in question or be useful in expanding one's network for the future.
- *Administrative and language skills* Research at EU level involves the filling in of research proposals, writing reports, books and so on in the English language. Interviews show that UK coordinators consider it an important element to have an English-speaking partner. Though this is hardly a determining factor, it is one of those invisible attributes that do count. Administrative experience of the kind relating to the filling in of proposal application forms and preparation of feasible budgets is another skill that a member of the project core is likely to have themselves or to find valuable in a key partner.
- *Reputation for influence* Some researchers are perceived as good 'door opening and gate keeping' partners, chosen not simply (if at all) for academic compatibility but for practical and political reasons. Sometimes this could amount to the favouring of a 'big name'. For example, 'Fran' (UK) chose a 'powerful' partner since a letter of introduction was required for the interviewing of key political authorities considered to be of importance for the research. Big names may also vastly improve the chances of getting funding. We have evidence of at least one case in which a coordinator designed the proposal entirely by himself, and then contacted a 'prestigious researcher' who himself admits that 'Kip basically just wanted to use me as a name'.
- *Positional reasons* At the other end of the spectrum, researchers may be contacted for such pragmatic reasons as their belonging to a southern European country. By EU rules, the involvement of such 'shotgun partners' would again improve funding prospects. 'Steve' (UK) recalls, 'I knew someone vaguely in Holland, picked up someone in Dublin by network, knew someone from Spain, Portugal and Greece' and acknowledged that success was more likely if a couple of Mediterranean partners joined in. On the other hand, for the shotgun partner, such calls could be perceived as unexpected 'manna from heaven' that helps them move forward in their own quest to stimulate or consolidate EU level participation.

The picture so far strongly suggests that EU partnerships are hierarchical in nature right from their very inception. It is worth noting, however, that situations where all partners are on a more or less equal footing do sometimes exist. An example is given by 'Martin' (UK): 'Liz was working on the paint industry. The Dutch coordinator contacted her and decided to do a comparative case study on the same industry. Liz met up with the Danish partner at a conference. There was a meeting to develop the proposal, which didn't include the Italians and Portuguese at this point. The Dutch coordinator was responsible for pulling them in at a later date .... But it took several years for the partnership to come to fruition. The project team came about through natural evolution over time, not put together just for DGXII. If the project bid wasn't successful, we would have aimed to get funding in some other way.' This kind of partnership built up over a relatively long period is likely to have the advantages of consolidation and stability during the course of the actual project. This issue brings us to the question of what happens in the career of an EU project once it has been set up.

The Dynamics of International Collaboration

Once a project has been approved for funding, the process of international collaboration enters its next, more intensive phase: that of actually doing the research. While the prospect of such collaboration is a very attractive feature of European involvement, various difficulties are known to arise in the concrete working and management of real projects.

There seems to be a more or less widely shared view that, while EU projects may be beneficial on the whole, some partners have to invest a lot more time than others in order to get the project up and running. Depending on the chain of outcomes, such investment may or may not be deemed productive. The coordinator may have a hard time finding the right people to work with. Other researchers face similar problems, if they are to find and train research assistants to work on the project. All these 'costs' are described by 'Steve' (UK): 'I think the problems have as much to do with the training of inexperienced researchers.... So, in fact, it created enormous demands particularly at the level of finding someone to work on it, because the other partners are working on it themselves, which was quite interesting, because for them it was directly related. We couldn't do it because we had too many projects. The demands of the travelling are a problem. I think at that level the time it takes to manage a project like this is much greater.'

Turning to the content of the work, the methodology might itself be controversial amongst partners, some wanting an open and free flowing approach and others preferring something fixed. For 'Mark' (UK), disagreements related closely to the sort of case studies and depth of analysis to be undertaken by the partners. 'Jane' (UK) gives the example of long discussions about basic concepts such as what constitutes a 'green space'. On the other hand, social environmental research being a relatively new area, some partners may be relatively unfamiliar with the topic under study, requiring a good deal of self-training in order to catch up. Depending on their other commitments and motivations, such background work may or may not be deemed worthwhile by these researchers. Controversies over method could similarly afflict relationships between main partners and their so-called 'junior' researchers who may not really be that junior in terms of their years of prior experience. From their academic training and past work, these research assistants could equally well have developed certain methodological and conceptual perspectives, which may not be easily discarded.

Another problem arising from the division of EU research labour between countries is associated with generation of comparable data. Here there may be genuine difficulties in translating the shared object of empirical study into the search for comparable representations across different countries. 'Fred' (UK) observes this difficulty in a project focusing on instruments/mechanisms for delivering sustainable development and the level of penetration of sustainability ideas into decision making: 'Some people had their own idea of what was a good case study, but others could not duplicate/get a corresponding one. So there was a problem of producing comparative information.' In our own research, we faced some early difficulties in having to deal with the fact that some countries simply do not have well-defined systems for social environmental research. On the other hand, such empirical troubles may turn out to constitute interesting and relevant findings in their own right.

Some researchers were quite critical about the added value provided by EU-funded research. For 'Fran' (UK), 'the gathering together of cross cultural studies, cases by national experts is not that illuminating, it does not generate new ideas, visions or agendas'. EU-funded research is deemed to be 'either too technical or narrow and could be done but it is of no interest, or else it is too loose, could be of interest but can't be done'. For 'Michel', it is precisely this diversity of partners in terms of discipline and, more specifically, the different research cultures in disciplines, which create great difficulty, as it is 'impossible to find common language of what the project is about'. So, in theory, the project is interdisciplinary, but in reality different perspectives are not sufficiently integrated, making the search for a common methodology rather futile. Finally, the great number of partners itself does not help as this implies more negotiation, and more conflict. So, for Michel, his EU involvement was a rather frustrating experience because of the different sets of people speaking different academic languages.

For 'Gary' (UK), 'interdisciplinary research is harder to carry out than single disciplinary research. Sometimes the ideas may be better but, on average, the outcomes are worse and it becomes quite difficult to find good interdisciplinary research.' This makes him adopt a sceptical position *vis à vis* EU research. For him, European projects are more about the creation of networks than the substantive content alone. For 'Steve' (UK), 'the problem with (country) case studies is that, because you are not doing them yourself, they are unreliable, and even though methodologically we've got this tight frame, it is not tight enough when it comes to writing papers'.

For some researchers, there is little added value from incorporating a European dimension into work. For example, 'Steve' (UK) argues that 'it is hard in the field of agricultural economics to give general prescriptions because the diversity in old landscapes with different geographical formations in Western Europe is immense'. In other cases, the European dimension may be central to the research question. For 'Vivien' (UK), a researcher focusing on issues of technological innovation in relation to environmental issues, the EU project permitted a move from the periphery to the core of the innovation studies field.

Finally, the usefulness and difficulties of working together with other researchers may depend on the stage of research at which collaboration takes place and also on its formal or informal character. While some researchers think a lot of intense collaboration early on is important, others believe that it is much more rewarding to work alone and collaborate at a later stage for mutual criticism and feedback. 'Steve' (UK) would be in this latter group. He believes that 'collaborating at earlier stages multiplies problems/work'. A much more informal, day-to-day, collaboration could be the right answer for these diseconomies of scale. The same researcher actually points out that, for him, 'collaboration takes place in the corridor, lunch, etc. that's what is healthy debate'. Obviously, there is no equivalent 'corridor' in which project members belonging to a virtual or distributed research team routinely meet, a point that underlines the institutional constraints of the setting in which international collaboration is situated.

CAREERS AND RESEARCH TRAJECTORIES

Having started with the variety of motivations that drive individuals towards involvement in EU social environmental research, we moved on to provide a flavour of the kinds of beliefs and social conventions that go into the making of the projects we studied. In this section, we turn these issues around and ask what happens to individuals once they have entered the system and find themselves in the business of navigating a maze of European networks. How does EU participation affect the development of individual careers? In turn, what are the typical career trajectories we observe across the EU research system? We focus below on two distinctive types occupying two ends of the social spectrum – the established and influential serial operators, and new, and typically junior, research assistants – while referring briefly to the experiences of researchers in the middle.

Serial Operators

In this book we have already alluded to the phenomenon whereby certain individuals are visibly and consistently active across several layers of the European research system. Such people are typically engaged in multiple projects, as well as being recurrent and prominent faces in the research policy context where new programmes are developed through workshops and advisory committees. Since such operators also tend to be part of other national and international environmental programmes and research initiatives, they are blessed with a broad range of 'the right' contacts. In the process, they become highly reputable figures who other researchers and research managers would like on their side. We call them 'serial operators'. Their prominence in the European social environmental research community can be attributed to major factors. First, other researchers recognize serial operators for their intellectual ability and/or as individuals who are well connected with other researchers and policy makers. Reputations created through past work in turn generate new invitations for participation in new projects, a phenomenon termed the 'Matthew effect' in the sociology of science (Merton, 1973).

Second, research managers treat serial operators as 'safe bets' when they evaluate new research proposals. Again, their reputation – which is likely to be further reinforced through renewed participation – helps justify further support, involvement and funding for these figures.

Turning to our database of SEER and Human Dimensions projects and researchers, we can now identify these serial operators in somewhat more precise fashion. We use two criteria: consistency of involvement indicated by participation in three or more projects, and active involvement in other international initiatives in social environmental research.

Serial involvement in EU projects

Of the 558 researchers on the EU database, only 27 (5 per cent) have been involved in three or more EU-funded projects (SEER and/or Human Dimensions). These individuals are mostly found in sociology or economics departments in universities and/or research centres focusing on issues such as environmental technology or valuation of environmental resources. Their distribution in the six countries we studied is shown in Table 3.1, which indicates that Dutch and UK researchers account for the majority of those who are especially well connected and networked.

Involvement in other international programmes

Of the 558 researchers on our database, 46 (8 per cent) either have been listed by DGXII as being important contacts in the field of social environmental

Table 3.1   Serial operators by country (involvement in EU projects)

Austria	1
Finland	0
Greece	1
Netherlands	4
Spain	1
UK	8

research or have been involved in one or more of the following initiatives and/or events. (We describe these initiatives in greater detail in Chapter 5.)

- The European Science Foundation's TERM (Tackling Environmental Resource Management) Programme. Committee members from phases 1 and 2 are included.
- The IHDP (International Human Dimensions Programme): members of the IHDP's Scientific Committee, as well as National Programme Committee contact persons and chairs of IHDP Science Project Committees, are included.
- The GIN (Greening of Industry Network). Members of both the Action Planning Committee and Advisory Board are included.
- A DGXII consultative workshop in Florence, a key meeting in setting the agenda of the first phase of the SEER programme.

Distribution of these researchers in our six countries is shown in Table 3.2, which reinforces the conclusion that most European serial operators in the world of social environmental research are from either the UK or the Netherlands. On our first criterion of involvement in EU projects, 80 per cent of these figures (12 out of 15) work in one of these countries; on the second criterion of participation in other international programmes, the figure is 75 per cent (18 out of 24).

Table 3.2   Serial operators by country (involvement in other international initiatives)

Austria	1
Finland	1
Greece	0
Netherlands	7
Spain	4
UK	11

Given these patterns of intensive participation, it is reasonable to conclude that there exists a group of elite researchers, and that this group is particularly influential in shaping the agenda of EU social environmental research. While the set of project coordinators – people who not only manage research, but also design the projects in the first place – is not identical to the group of serial operators, we can also consider their distribution by country for further confirmation on this matter. From our database, we find that almost 90 per cent of all projects had a UK or Dutch coordinator, again putting researchers from these countries in the role of key agenda setters. While the number of Spanish partners in projects is relatively large, Spanish researchers as project coordinators are few and far between. Spanish, as well as Greek, researchers seem to be responding to a research agenda developed by others.

Project coordinators tend to develop multiple identities. On the one hand, they must negotiate with other partners on the everyday problems of collaboration. On the other, they also have a reputation to maintain or enhance *vis à vis* research managers and, possibly, users, which may require redirecting the partners' contributions. This is quite clearly perceived by 'Steve' (UK): 'I said to the coordinator that it was hard to write something that did not strike the contrasts rather than comparisons and he said we don't want contrasts because we want to run European policy.'

The challenges of coordinating an interdisciplinary project and network are keenly perceived by some of our interviewees. For 'Pat' (UK), it involves a loss of both freedom and flexibility. Coordination requires specific skills. It does not only relate to the ability to negotiate different demands from the partners, but, more importantly, to the ability to integrate the bits and pieces into a coherent product. 'Fred' (UK) remarks that 'It is (relatively) easy to coordinate, but the problem is not having breadth of expertise, so integration becomes difficult. It is a nightmare for coordinators to get commonality.'

Whether as project coordinators or as influential advisors, these serial operators clearly occupy a key position in shaping the agenda of the social environmental research field. Through this, they are also able to advance their own careers. However, prospects for hegemonic capture of the field are tempered by the fact that this elite necessarily relies on a wide range of players for doing European research. The tensions and dilemmas engendered by working in research teams are especially illustrated in the case of research assistants who, in most projects of this kind, are responsible for carrying out much of the work on the ground.

Research Assistants

The picture of EU participation and its implications for career trajectories looks significantly different when we consider research assistants in general and junior researchers in particular. Although different institutional contexts make for different sets of incentives for junior researchers across Europe, there still exists a set of common issues arising from the precarious, unstable work situations they frequently share even as they go about the business of doing the bulk of the actual research.

As in other cases, a certain reputation may well account for the beginning of their involvement in EU social environmental research projects; for example, in the form of a reference provided to the principal researcher by a former employer whose judgment may be particularly valued. In other cases, the junior may already be part of a research team built around the principal researcher. In such instances, they are likely to be involved in the setting up of the project. Finally, a more random response to relevant job advertisements on the Internet, or in journals and newspapers, represents a third way of getting involved.

Motives for responding positively when contacted are not as varied as in the case of more established researchers. In many occasions, the junior does not have a real choice: they either take the job or remain in a precarious position. For all the other glaring differences in their national systems, junior researchers in both the UK and Spain describe this kind of scenario. EU funds provide them with the opportunity to do a PhD thesis around the specific theme of the project or related issues. Or, as with more senior researchers, the job could allow them a point of entry into an area of interest that is unrecognized in their home disciplines.

But engagement in EU social environmental research simultaneously generates a different set of career problems for these research assistants. Interdisciplinary research, common to most EU projects, makes for a challenging experience. On the one hand, the learning process itself is deemed a very positive feature of projects which do not have a 'home discipline'. Personal contacts with other researchers and the feeling of being part of a research team are also positive. But, on the other hand, research assistants may be left feeling insecure and confused as they are obliged to lose part of their disciplinary identity – if they have one – in favour of an interdisciplinary tradition which has yet to become accepted in research evaluation procedures and reward systems.

Whether or not the researcher profits from a permanent position in the research centre becomes quite relevant when considering the advantages provided by the project. For juniors and intermediate 'have-nots', European projects might simply mean employment opportunities. Sometimes this might mean having to patch together a salary from pieces of work on different projects. Thus, even though a 'save the environment' type of personal commitment tended to be common among the junior group, it is sometimes transformed as these individuals make their way through the system: as with 'Dale' (UK) who chronicles his own shift from naïveté to a 'more hard-nosed and realistic' attitude about working 'with the economic and political systems we have'.

BOX 3.6

'Joan' (UK) says, 'Yes, I feel very strange being in a planning department. It was really strange at the start, but now I've come to realise that planning is all-embracing as geography can be. But I do feel quite a sense of a loss of identity because I did class myself as an environmental scientist, and now I don't really know what I am anymore. But I'm hoping to use the work from this project in a PhD.'

BOX 3.7

'Steve' (UK) observes: 'The European project gives T employment. Is that important? It is for them [other project partners] and it would have been for us if we hadn't got other projects. The employment it would have given would have employed S, but because we've got a whole load of other projects it became less important.'

Apart from this, junior researchers benefit from the training obtained through the project leading in many cases to a PhD thesis around the project theme (as noted above), and thereby creating new research capacity in the field. Involvement in EU projects is quite prestigious and useful when applying for jobs in universities or research centres.

BOX 3.8

'Steve' (UK) describes the advantages for the junior researchers in his project: 'The project has had an enormous amount of significance for her. She's registered for a PhD around it and once the project is finished she is almost certainly going to do a PhD full time, if we can get the funding and she is putting in an application today to the university. It will change her life ... It will have contributed to the building up of a research capacity quite significantly, and the space it gives her.'

Projects and Career Trajectories

Coordinators have a certain advantage in terms of a capacity to chart a coherent career trajectory for themselves. Since they design the proposal, they are in a position to ensure that its content connects with their previous work. At the same time, since they already have an established reputation, they can equally well venture into new, uncharted territory, which may be of interest to them for a host of intellectual, strategic or institutional reasons. Unfamiliarity with the topic is not necessarily the hurdle it might be for lesser-known researchers. At least for those coordinators with a reputation already built up over previous work, displaying a lack of knowledge in a specific area will by no means detract from their status. Instead, they have the flexibility to contact people with the right sort of background and to enlist new players into the emerging project.

For those partners drawn into an already existing agenda, the project may or may not be a departure from past work. In cases where the substantive topic remains the same, there is sometimes a discontinuity in the methodology employed. For 'Rob' (UK), their research 'is only loosely based on things we had done before, the methodology is quite different from what we had been doing before. The case study ... has been modified in a sense to fit into DGXII requirements as I wouldn't have carried out the project as it is now.' In the case of Spanish researchers participating in EU projects, we find that many had already done research on issues related to the project theme. This reflects the fact that they are contacted not solely for their 'southern component' but also because of their substantive reputations: for example, one 'Juan' is known as 'Mr macroeconomic energy and resource analyst' in Spain.

Researchers renowned in a certain area of social science, but who have never undertaken social environmental work before, may sometimes be contacted to apply their specialized knowledge to environmental issues. Certain fields are naturally more amenable than others to the making of such an extension. One good example is work on the economics of technological change that has come to be applied to environmental issues. In this case the 'environment' adds a new dimension to past work, but does not necessarily represent a theme for the future. 'Jack' (UK) gives his reasons why 'social environmental research is not [his] thing unless it has something to do with environmental technology. It is a diversion for me .... It would be a waste of time to apply for anything environmental.'

Finally, there also seems to be a relationship between not enjoying a permanent position in research institutes (that is, being a 'have-not') and developing a transdisciplinary background. The less networked and less stable the situation of the researcher, the greater the likelihood of joining different projects, leading to the further loss of disciplinary roots and the creation of a 'transdisciplinary' identity. For example, 'Liz' (UK) reports that she is 'not very well networked as [this] is relatively new research [for me] .... It seems that the future is really from one contract to another and (my) disciplinary identity is unformed.'

While these issues are perhaps typical of a new field in the making, they illustrate the diversity of levels of seniority involved. Nonetheless, European social environmental research has positioned itself as a useful and interesting domain for a number of people whose academic identities have developed and can be expected to evolve in the future.

MAKING ORDER

We have already discussed at length how individuals navigate the research system in different ways and for different reasons. Some strategies are, however, much more deliberate than others and, thus, have a more direct influence on the evolution of research agendas of the research institutions and programmes at national level. The point is that, by engaging in those strategies, some individuals act as intermediaries between the EU and the national level, and help in the mutual dissemination of new research ideas and issues.

The role of serial operators is worth mentioning in this regard. More than any other group, they move between different levels, apply for EU funds and, at the same time, may be called to participate in a project funded by national sources. Depending on how well connected they happen to be, their influence on agendas may be more or less direct, and more or less successful. 'Carlos' (Spain) is a case of one well-connected and sought-out person, who has tried but failed to get his research area (ecological history and environmental justice) onto the EU research programme. He has, however, been able to influence the Latin American research agenda in social environmental issues.

Some individuals, by engaging in EU research, are also able to determine their own institution's research agenda. 'Sam' (UK) believes that he has set up a broader European dimension at his institute, which had a marked UK orientation before he became involved. Networking funds have primarily driven this, with two or three fairly large European research projects whose impact is said to have been considerable. His influence seems to have lasted even after his departure from the place.

Taking account of the versatile, many-sided character of researchers, we see that they do not only respond to the research agenda but also shape it in one way or another. It is against this background that the evolution of the European social environmental research agenda described in the next chapter must be read. While we will show that social environmental research in the European Union has converged around a fairly narrow set of technocratic issues, it is important to keep in mind that this agenda has not so much been imposed as negotiated through interaction between an informal community of influential researchers and research managers.

4. The evolution of ideas

INTRODUCTION

Since its launch in 1991, EU-funded social environmental research has more or less converged around a technocratic concern with the development of policy tools. This relatively narrow focus belies the broad set of expectations about the contribution of the social sciences with which the research programme was announced. In this chapter, we elaborate on the nature of this shift and argue that the agenda for research has both influenced and been strongly influenced by the European political–economic project of *ecological modernization*. The central proposition behind ecological modernization is that, rather than pulling in opposite directions, programmes for economic growth and environmental protection can be made to work to each other's benefit. From being a key concept that emerged out of social research on environmental policy reform, ecological modernization is now both the overarching response to environmental degradation and a central theme shaping the course of European research on the subject. Yet the existence of such a broad consensus does not tell the whole story.

Studies in the sociology of knowledge have consistently found a tension between the shared frameworks and concepts of formal scientific discourse and the divergent realities of actual scientific work. An equally compelling finding from political science is that, in the practicalities of its implementation, policy often departs significantly from the formalities of its construction. How then are consensus and heterogeneity reconciled in practice? The extended literature on actor–network theory in the sociology of science offers the analytic concept of *boundary objects* in response to this question. Boundary objects, whether abstract or concrete, are 'plastic enough to adapt to local needs and the constraints of several parties employing them, yet robust enough to maintain a common identity across sites' (Star and Griesemer, 1989, p. 393).

In the following analysis of the dynamics of EU social environmental research, we argue that the discourse of ecological modernization has served as one such object. Different conceptions of what counts as 'the environment', of the role that the social sciences are expected to play (and that social scientists may see themselves playing) and of the very idea of European 'policy-relevant' research have all been subsumed under the common rubric of 'ecological modernization'. The idea of ecological modernization is not only simple and powerful in its reach, but also vague in its specification. Its vagueness is precisely why it is highly adaptable to a variety of interests, while still serving to make them coherent in their joint capacity.

In this chapter we analyse the evidence that the ecological modernization project for reform has played a significant part in the way that policy has developed and in the way research has been undertaken for the European Commission and for various national governments. We suggest that the project has provided the essential, often unstated, intellectual bearings for the research activities of DGXII, and especially for social environmental research. The chapter is organized in six sections.

We begin with an overview of the policy discourse and practice of ecological modernization as summarized in the recent social science literature on the topic. We then argue that ecological modernization is central to the political project of creating a unified Europe, using the OECD Technology and Environment Programme (1990–93) to illustrate the point. The third section explores the way in which environmental policy has appropriated ecological modernization principles in different national environments. In the fourth section we discuss the evidence that the paradigm of ecological modernization has significantly influenced research activities at the European level in particular, and in some national systems. In this context, we trace the evolution and narrowing of DGXII's social environmental research agenda. Next, drawing on the concept of 'boundary objects', we attempt to explain how the research agenda has been distilled in this fashion from a multiplicity of conflicting ideas, disciplinary approaches and assumptions. We conclude with a critique of ecological modernization, focusing on its failure to address questions of equity in any substantive fashion even as it claims to reconcile economic, environmental and social objectives.

ECOLOGICAL MODERNIZATION

For the purposes of this overview, it is worth starting by distinguishing between two usages of 'ecological modernization', namely the theory proposed and developed in environmental sociology circles, and the policy practice as observed and described in these and wider circles. In the following sections, we will examine the ways in which ecological modernization theory and practice are converging, and identify some of the gaps, criticisms and tensions entailed therein.

'Ecological modernization', unlike 'cleaner technologies' or 'sustainable development', is not yet a catch phrase as such in policy practice. As identified by various theorists and researchers, ecological modernization represents the evolution of several ideas in a way that has allowed appropriation under different political ideological frameworks: conservative, social-democratic and liberal. In fact it could be said to represent an attempt to bring several, until now opposing, ideas 'under the same hat' (Luhmann 1989). It may be read in the process of institutionalization of the environmentalist movement (Eder, 1996; Jamison, 1996). It is reflected in developments in environmental economics across the range of neoclassical, institutional and radical traditions (Deblonde, 1996; Mulberg, 1996), not least in the evolution of environmental policies at the national and EU level.

Ecological modernization theory has been discussed in a variety of publications (Simonis, 1989; Spaargaren and Mol, 1992; Weale, 1992; Janicke, 1988; Hajer, 1997; Gouldson and Murphy, 1996). Through the course of this theoretical elaboration, ecological modernization has come to mean the following:

- that environmental degradation associated with industrial activities can be turned around by industrial innovation of the sort that leads to the adoption of 'cleaner' technologies and associated organizational processes;
- that such innovation can be a new way of improving industrial competitiveness and creating economic growth;
- that the modernization of production can be complemented by the rise of environmentally conscious patterns of consumption in the market-place;
- that this positive linkage of environment and economy can be assisted and nurtured through the appropriate national and European policies.

Spaargaren (1997) takes Joseph Huber's (1982; 1985) concept of 'switch-over' as the starting point for conceptual clarification. Huber discerned a process of environmental policy reform, largely initiated in the early 1980s, which combined a long-term vision of socioeconomic change with a set of short-term changes associated with technological innovation. The long-term changes imply institutional reform, and are heavily dependent on convergence in European policy. They also depend upon a willingness to intervene in both environmental policy and industrial policy, through the policy instruments available to the European Union. Huber's basic premise and argument is that 'the dynamics of capitalism can ... be made to work in the direction of sustainable production and consumption' (Spaargaren, 1997, p. 16).

Gouldson and Murphy point out that ecological modernization assumes the possibility of a *synergy* between environmental protection and economic development, notwithstanding the conflicts assumed in the past (Gouldson and Murphy, 1996). In this analysis, the prime mover is government, which helps to provide a broader context than is usually provided by environmental policy alone. It also implies the creation of new products and services that demonstrate improved environmental and economic performance.

According to Hajer (1997), ecological modernization is distinct from the two main opposing paradigms that dominated environmental discourse prior to the early 1980s. On the one hand, the radical ecological paradigm claimed that the ecological crisis could only be overcome through sweeping change in the means of production. On the other hand, what Hajer (ibid., p. 248) calls the 'pragmatic legal–administrative response' advocated 'remedial' or 'end-of-pipe' solutions and standards for improving environmental quality.

The radical ecological project underpinned many environmental grassroots movements that emerged in reaction to major infrastructure projects. These represented both an attempt to protect local spaces from environmental degradation caused by infrastructure projects (industrial sites, transport projects and so on) based on a 'not in my back yard' (NIMBY) reaction, and at the same time a voice of protest against the central state administration and major capitalist interests. Environmental regulation was in many cases the state response to these conflicts, attempting to pacify concerned citizens through the introduction of relevant legislation at the national or international level. Yet it remained opposed to the radical ecological project mainly by reason of its keeping faith with the principles of economic growth and its view of environmental problems as externalities that can be 'fixed' after the fact.

In the event, even the environmental movements and green parties came to realize that the environmental issue was not enough to guarantee political mobilization (less so political support in elections) over time. For one thing, many of the specific projects to which environmental movements were opposed had not only negative environmental externalities but also positive economic benefits accruing to the regions which were not so easy to overlook.

Towards the end of the 1980s, a new mentality or discourse emerged. This has been marked by a turn towards the development of so-called 'clean' (later 'cleaner') technologies in production, and a claim to pursue long-term strategies of prevention in place of short-term, remedial or 'end-of-pipe' solutions to problems that had already been created. Further, this concern with cleaner products and services is only one facet of a wider orientation in research and policy towards empowering consumers to make environmentally friendly choices. The simultaneous transformation of consumption alongside production is expected to come about through the provision of information that is supposed to enable consumers to change their buying and resource-using habits.

How this change came about is still a story that needs to be told. It seems to have been the culmination of a number of factors: the gradual 'greening' of politics, with the establishment of green parties in a number of countries and the adoption of green issues in the agendas of the traditional parties; the failure of grassroots environmental movements to sustain political mobilization and translate it into radical political action; the failure of environmental regulation to record substantial positive results; and the gradual emergence of 'green' marketing strategies in industry, coupled with the opening up of a new professional lobby of environmental consultants and engineers.

So far we have drawn on ecological modernization theory to describe the emergence of the political discourse and practice of ecological modernization. In the next section we focus specifically on the role of ecological modernization within the process of Europeanization.

ECOLOGICAL MODERNIZATION AND EUROPEAN ENVIRONMENTAL POLICY

In arguing that ecological modernization is central to the European project as a whole, we mean the following. The European project aims for a convergence in the use of materials and energy flows within EU countries, buttressed by regulatory frameworks that place Europe on a competitive footing with North America and Japan. By taking the initiative in 'cleaner' production methods and greener fiscal policies – and, thus, in the modernization of production itself – the European region is expected to become simultaneously more competitive in the global economy. This objective is at once radical and conservative in that it implies a conscious shaping of European industry, but one that can be accommodated within late capitalism without serious difficulty. These twin goals are reflected in the development of the OECD's 1990–93 Programme on Technology and the Environment, the main purpose of which was to understand the relationship between economic growth and environmental sustainability with a view to 'indicating how technological change, environmental preservation and rational natural resource management can reinforce each other' (OECD, 1992).

This OECD programme was launched to promote the implementation, innovation and diffusion of 'cleaner technologies', focusing specifically on the role of government in this regard. Within this framework, a self-assessment guide was proposed as an evaluation instrument to be used by governments to identify the advantages and disadvantages of specific policy mechanisms as well as for promoting discussions on the subject amongst various parties. Through this, the aim was to bring about a 'preventive' approach to the environment in place of fragmented and 'reactive' strategies.

A preventive approach to environmental sustainability is necessarily one that requires the involvement of a whole chain of production and consumption practices. This in turn requires the participation of a range of economic and social actors, including the public. In policy terms, the integrated character of preventive solutions was translated into information provision programmes and strategies for cleaner production. The latter was felt to be a paradigmatic change in technology use and development. According to the OECD's working definition:

> cleaner production is meant to reduce the amounts of energy and raw materials based on natural resources needed to produce, market and use products. At the same time, production, marketing and disposal of these products should also be such that releases of potentially harmful contaminants to environmental media are kept as low as practicable. (Ibid., p. 4)

Within this framework, 'cleaner technology' is an umbrella term covering all those technological instruments which effect environmental sustainability by focusing on energy use across the life cycle of a product, right up to the point of its disposal.

Underpinning the OECD Technology and the Environment Programme are the following ideological assumptions.

- Economic growth is the basis for the creation, maintenance and improvement of the standard of living.
- Economic growth relies on technological innovation and adaptation.
- Economic growth is mediated through the market and reflected in the pattern of competitiveness of individual economic actors.
- The quality of the natural environment is a basic premise for human survival and natural resources are neither inexhaustible nor resistant to damage and degradation.
- In societies that define the quality of life via economic growth, techno-logical innovation is likewise the means for ensuring the quality of the environment.
- Technological change, if conceptualized and implemented in unsustain-able fashion, may produce a backlash in terms of life standards via its effects on the environment.

Against these background assumptions, the OECD Programme is framed in terms of the belief that technological innovation can create an optimum or near-to-optimum interaction between the economy and the environment, and between efficiency and effectiveness (and, as of late, equity). The question then becomes how best to stimulate and/or regulate technological development in order to ensure such a positive-sum interaction. At the political level, the emphasis is placed on pragmatism: both prevention and repair solutions are needed; there can be no immediate short-term solution; hence, also, the gradual shift from the use of the term 'clean technologies' towards the use of the term 'clean*er* tech-nologies' and 'best available technologies'. At the level of policy, an integrated approach, that is, a combination of command and control measures with economic instruments and knowledge-based instruments (including research), is preferred.

The above discussion shows that all those themes identified in environmental sociology as pivotal to the project of ecological modernization are illustrated in the discourse of the OECD Programme on Technology and the Environment. Given this ideology, how then are specific environmental policy instruments to be chosen and assessed? The programme postulates the twin criteria of (economic) efficiency and (environmental) effectiveness. Needless to say, the attempt to strike an optimal balance between efficiency and effectiveness (especially in the short term) is hardly straightforward. Further, it is hindered by deficiencies in our knowledge base regarding environmental sustainability and economic growth. Consequently, one may expect to observe in the formulation and application of environmental policies either (a) the prevalence of compromise solutions in the short to medium term which are a priori unsatisfying both in terms of effectiveness and in terms of efficiency, or (b) an emphasis either on the dimension of effectiveness or on that of efficiency which involves a decision of political choice but which is, subsequently, likely to inspire reactionary strategies.

If, as we have seen, ecological modernization has taken centre-stage in the broad development of policy in Europe, to what extent has it been influential in the making of national environmental policy in different countries? We find that the earliest thinking along the lines of this paradigm originated in the Netherlands. Given the close interaction between Dutch researchers and policy managers in their own country as well as in Europe (see Chapter 2), we begin to see the pattern of flow of these influential ideas from one national level to the European level and, in turn, back to other national contexts.

ECOLOGICAL MODERNIZATION AND NATIONAL ENVIRONMENTAL POLICY

The Netherlands and the UK

The development of environmental policy in the Netherlands exemplifies the trends towards ecological modernization. One of the first nations to formulate an environmental policy back in 1971, the Netherlands established a separate agency for that purpose and began to consider how environmental concerns might be incorporated into various policy sectors. As the environment gained in public attention in the 1970s, environmental policy became a rewarding issue for politicians and the stage was set for its institutionalization. In the

1980s, the emphasis in policy began to shift from command and control instruments and regulatory standards towards 'achieving (environmental) goals' via a new responsiveness to industrial interests. Here we observe the beginnings of ecological modernization ideas.

Published in 1988 and arguing that the state of the environment was dramatically deteriorating, a report entitled *Concerns for Tomorrow* came close to sparking a real public controversy. This was forestalled by the Dutch government's First National Environmental Policy Plan. As well as identifying major target areas for environmental policy, this plan put forward the idea of an 'optimal policy-mix of policy instruments' for environmental problems, a mix which would 'assure the support of key actors or target groups for these measures'. It also strongly emphasized the role of consumers as citizens entitled to information but also responsible for relevant action, and the role of harmonization of goals with 'partner countries': An explicit reference to 'sustainability' as a goal was a hallmark of the Second National Environmental Policy Plan in 1994.

Aided by media publicity and the Dutch Priority Programme on Acidification, acid rain became a crucial lever in the development of Dutch environmental policy. In his comparative study of the response to acid rain in the Netherlands and the UK, Hajer notes how ecological modernization became the 'only discourse in which actors could credibly express their concerns and priorities' (Hajer, 1997, p. 251). This in turn brought about major institutional changes in the Netherlands, including a centralization of environmental policy and a redrawing of the accommodative practices characteristic of the Dutch system of government. Despite the establishment of a central Environmental Ministry in 1971, the provinces exerted control over environmental policy decisions. This was to change in the mid-1980s, following the perception of an 'environmental crisis' and the endorsement of ecological modernization as a source of ideas and strategies with which to tackle that crisis.

In the UK, on the other hand, the acid rain problem produced two competing 'story lines': traditional–pragmatist and ecomodernist. As in Dutch environmental policy of the 1970s, the traditional style of regulation in the UK was accommodative rather than adversarial. Within the story line of this old 'traditional–pragmatist' regime, the acid rain problem was framed as a question for research. Within the new 'ecomodernist' story line, acid rain was identified as an issue of wider relevance demanding new and radical policy interventions even in the absence of complete and undisputed scientific evidence (ibid., pp. 114–19). However, ecological modernization ideas could not gain as wide a support as was found in the Netherlands, and the result was 'a continued legitimacy of old regulatory arrangements' (ibid., p. 161). More generally, Britain has been a comparative latecomer in environmental policy, despite the fact that British environmental legislation has a very long history dating back to the nineteenth century.

Until the mid-1980s, UK environmental legislation was built up piecemeal in response to particular environmental problems. Environmental policy more generally was characterized by an ad hoc improvisation and a confusing assortment of institutions and laws. The basis of environmental controls lay in land-use planning, much of it operated by local governments. In general, the organization and implementation of environmental policies was devolved to local authorities or semi-independent inspectorates. At the time, the Department of the Environment believed that, since the problems of pollution are experienced first within the confines of particular localities, the primary responsibility for dealing with them should rest with the relevant local authorities.

The continuing focus on the local level contributed to the failure to develop a strategic vision on the environment, as in the Netherlands, but on the other hand it empowered mobilization at the grassroots level. Environmental groups proliferated, particularly in the voluntary sector, but they were largely concerned with wildlife conservation, public access and amenity. Membership of some of these organizations, for example, the Royal Society for the Protection of Birds and the National Trust, was very high. The local focus also contributed to the strengthening of the scientific discourse (and hence, of what Hajer calls the 'traditional–pragmatist' story line) insofar as agencies responsible for environmental quality control were often divorced from the civil service structure, and staffed by professional scientists and engineers.

In the UK, the appropriation of ecological modernization principles in environmental policy came about more gradually and through Europeanization. Although the UK has had considerable influence in international environmental policy, its contribution to the European domain has been largely procedural rather than substantive. Europeanization has resulted in a codification of the UK's flexible administrative style of regulation, the legal specification of environmental standards and a shifting of power away from local government towards a variety of private sector bodies, agencies and central government departments.

The comparison of the development of environmental policies in the UK and the Netherlands is of particular interest precisely because of the different ways in which the ecological modernization principles were appropriated. Two themes in particular stand out. First, it would seem that the so-called 'negotiated compliance model' which has been promoted under the ecological modernization banner as a 'new' way of doing politics is not that new after all. Not only has this model been characteristic of Dutch politics over decades, rooted in the specific political culture of that country ('pillarization'), but it also characterized the early days of British environmental policy. The principal desire of policy makers in Britain until the early 1980s, at least, was to ensure the cooperation of those most affected by legislation. This involved the extensive use of voluntary procedures and forms of self-regulation, as well as 'consider-able latitude in the drawing up of regulations to allow for negotiated compliance' (Lowe and Ward, 1998, p. 8). Informal regulation was combined with close consultation with all affected interest groups. In sum, the United Kingdom had a consensual and technical approach to policy making, coupled with a concern for the practicality of legislation and a strong desire to avoid imposing solutions.

Second, if we look at the specific policy packages that emerged in the 1990s in both countries, the differences are not significant despite the divergent approaches. This is less of a surprise perhaps for the UK which, after all, made no pretence about adopting a 'new' discourse. The Netherlands, on the other hand, experienced something of a legitimation crisis, due to 'the fact that the ecomodernist discourse-coalition combined the active promotion of an apocalyptic depiction of the problem with the endorsement of a policy package that fell seriously short of its own goals' (Hajer, 1997, p. 252). This leads Hajer to conclude that the point is not so much that existing regulatory mechanisms failed to solve the acid rain problem, as that environmental policy practices in general aim to make environmental problems manageable within the structures of industrial society.

Austria

Acid rain also dominated the Austrian environmental policy scene in the 1980s. However, the beginnings of national environmental policy were rather different from those in the Netherlands or the UK. They can be traced to the opening of a nuclear reactor at Zwetendorf which resulted in a referendum in 1978. This referendum spelled the end of nuclear energy in Austria and provided the Ministry of Environment (established in 1972) with the necessary momentum for the formulation of policies. Command and control instruments, mainly legislation and the setting of standards, dominated the Austrian environmental policy scene in the 1980s. The 1990s marked the emergence of attempts to develop more comprehensive approaches which emphasized the diffusion of 'cleaner technologies' within the framework of sustainable development.

The possibility of using a referendum to arrest political decisions is charac-teristic of Austrian political culture which emphasizes, like the Netherlands, negotiation and appropriation. The 'social partnership' model of decision making requires that all policy proposals be approved by the main interest groups, namely, trade unions representing workers' interests, and the Chamber of Commerce and Association of Industrialists representing employer and economic interests, respectively. In developing the National Environmental Plan, this circle was enlarged to include NGOs and the research community.

Like the Netherlands, Austria was quick to adopt the discourse of ecological modernization. Environmental management continues to be centralized in the context of legal standard setting and in the codification of implementation procedures. However, the emphasis on the regional dimension of sustainability continues to exist in environmental policy, as in the research programmes on 'islands of sustainability' and 'cultural landscapes' discussed in Chapter 2. This regional focus brings out another problematic dimension of the ecological modernization discourse, namely the relation of the global to the local.

Southern Europe

However inspirational, the call to 'think globally, act locally' raises a set of new questions concerning the management of environmental problems. It often makes clear the mismatch between goals and policy instruments previously noted, and forces recognition of the point that successful implementation of environmental policy depends on local actors, including citizens. Perhaps more importantly, it shows that the problem of environmental policy is not so much one of codification of standards through centralization, but rather one of co-ordination of action and reflexive policy making.

The notion of regional sustainability also raises the question of equity. Redclift and Sage (1994, p. 499) note that, from the perspective of developing countries, distributive issues have always been at the heart of debate on global environmental change. Further, there are two dimensions to equity, namely, intragenerational and intergenerational equity.

> The first emphasises existing differences between countries, and within this generation; the second emphasises the temporal dimension, differences between this and future generations. The concern of most commentators in the North has been with future generations of 'people', although this is usually implicit, while that of those in the South has been with the current generation. (Ibid., pp. 502–3)

This gap in perspective exists not only between 'North' and 'South' – (the advanced industrialized societies and the developing world) but between southern and eastern parts of Europe. In southern and eastern Europe the emphasis is clearly on the modernization side of ecological modernization. Here, the argument of 'needing to catch up' with the richer and more advanced northern neighbours is often heard in discussions about the environment. This is coupled with a comparatively weak environmental movement. Hence, for southern European countries like Spain and Greece, the main lever for environmental policy promotion has been entry into the European Union. This has implied the adoption of a number of directives regarding the environment, the most important being the introduction of environmental impact assessment. In eastern European countries, similar processes can be observed in relation to the process of accession and the adoption of the so-called Environment Acquis (European Commission, 1998a).

Evaluating Greece's institutional response to sustainable development, Fousekis and Lekakis (1997) point out an ambivalence with the term 'sustainable development' as indicated by the combined use of three terms (*aeiforiki* v. *viosimi* v. *ypostiriksimi*), the meanings of which are similar but distinct. They conclude that the Greek response has been 'limited, partial and fragmented' and that it does not even correspond to 'acknowledgement by cosmetic compliance' (ibid., p. 149). Problems with operationalizing an environmental strategy in Greece are further exacerbated by a multiplicity of relevant players, even at the state level. In the official documents of the Commission this problem has been referred to as one of 'transposition' rather than 'implementation', yet this national-level problem may not be that different from the difficulties surrounding the implementation of international agreements (Tronner and Penker, 1999).

Looking back on the flow of 'ecological modernization' ideas across different national contexts, we find that the principles were first formalized as an explicit discourse seeking to accommodate environment and economy in the Netherlands. From here, ecological modernization came to be adopted as a central plank of European policy. Through the influence of Europeanization, environmental policy in both Austria and the UK also came to reflect this discourse. However, in the case of the UK, ecological modernization does not signal a significant departure in actual policy practice which has traditionally been consensual and accommodative in nature. Ecological modernization, as a discourse, represents the explicit codification of these practices rather than something new. In Austria, on the other hand, the discourse has been adapted into a predominantly regional context. Finally, in the southern European countries, we find that questions of equity generate a significant clash between the generic ideas of ecological modernization and problems of regional sustainability.

In the next section, we move on to consider the influence of ecological modernization on the agenda of European social environmental research.

ECOLOGICAL MODERNIZATION AND SOCIAL ENVIRONMENTAL RESEARCH

European Agendas

The production of new research is pivotal to the task of implementing the ecological modernization project. It is therefore not surprising to discover that the ideas of ecological modernization have become etched in the agenda for European social environmental research. In this section, we trace the evolution of the EU research agenda from the first call for papers (1991) to the Fourth Framework Programme (1996), concluding with a few observations on the Fifth Framework Programme which was launched during the time this volume was written. We focus on three key aspects of the agenda – the substance of the research agenda, the role of social science in the context of the environment, and the meaning of policy relevance in research – and explore the ways in which these have changed. Our picture is based on a survey of the sequence of meetings, calls for proposals, applications and projects which together make up the body of EU-funded social environmental research.

In 1990, the EU organized an agenda-setting workshop in Florence; this was the springboard for the development of the Socio-Economic Environmental Research Programme (SEER). The workshop was structured in recognizably *disciplinary* terms. By this we mean that participants were invited to reflect on the difference the environment made to their own area of social scientific expertise. Following various stages of revisions, the work programme which emerged invited proposals under four headings:

1. the relationship between the human being and nature,
2. environmental policy implementation and monitoring,
3. environmental problems in an international perspective,
4. methodological and epistemological research of importance for environmental problems and policies.

The first theme points towards contributions from psychology, sociology, anthropology and philosophy, disciplines which could be expected to shed light on environmental values and consciousness, beliefs and attitudes towards nature, and their dynamics. The second theme treats policy as an area of expertise within political science, economics and law, the expectation being that new analytic approaches to economic development and environmental costs could be developed, and methods of assessment made more integrated through the introduction of a cultural perspective. The emphasis is heavily on evaluation and assessment as the proper role for social science in relation to policy; however, a hint of the shift to come can be seen in references to the need for new policy tools and technologies. While the third theme, oriented towards transboundary policy, aims to draw from the discipline of international relations, there is, likewise, a whiff of ecological modernization ideas in its defining the task of improving Europe's position in international negotiations as a challenge. The final theme refers to broad questions about the relationship between science and policy, including fundamental concerns such as uncertainty and cultural meanings associated with knowledge. In the event, few proposals were submitted under this more open heading and the theme fell by the wayside as subsequent calls came to focus on the instrumental purpose of improving science for policy.

Considering the early SEER agenda in toto, we find 'the environment' framed in broad terms so that it refers to 'nature' rather than merely a set of sectors such as agriculture, transport, energy, waste or pollution. 'Policy' is likewise construed in terms of generic *pathways* towards a sustainable society; but this later became translated into detailed representations of particular instruments and measures, and the need for their assessment.

The SEER Programme's first call for proposals stimulated a number of comparative research project applications – for example, comparisons of cultural meanings of the environment or of the implementation of an EU policy across different European countries – many of which were located within particular disciplines or traditions. These included psychology, political science and game theory, but surprisingly few from economics.

The range of work commissioned in Phase 2 of the SEER Programme (1993) begins to show signs, both in the call for proposals and submitted projects, of a narrowing agenda. The notion that social science disciplines can play a valuable role in their own right wanes in the process. Some of the original headings have become more strictly defined, as, for example, 'strategies and indicators for pathways to sustainability', 'global and regional environmental issues' and 'the role of R&D in and for policy'. New themes focus on environmental issues as they relate to specific sectors (tourism, transport, cities) or lay out already identified problems for policy such as 'uncertainty' and 'lack of trust' in government. The relationship between economic growth and environmental sustainability is still seen in terms of a need for *balance*, rather than the possibility of *synergy*. However, research submissions in this round introduce the questions of life cycle assessment and clean technologies, thereby paving the way for a more wholesale shift in thinking along the lines of ecological modernization.

By 1996, SEER had been relabelled the 'Human Dimensions' element of the Environment and Climate Programme, itself a part of the EU-wide Fourth Framework Programme for research (European Commission, 1996). A review of the 1994–8 catalogue of projects confirms the drift towards the technocratic agenda of ecological modernization. All the project abstracts underline policy relevance and application, and most disguise their origin in any specific discipline or research tradition of social science. 'Policy', in this case, is about developing tools at many different levels – local, sectoral, national, regional – rather than about more cross-cutting pathways. The shift towards sectoral issues in the framing of the environment is especially evident: rather than seeing environment as 'nature', the core themes are 'transport', 'water' and 'waste', as well as 'clean technology' and 'business transformation'.

Projects funded in the first sub-area of the Human Dimensions programme dealt with charting the social, economic and institutional conditions under which 'innovative' environmental management approaches could be successfully implemented, the underlying objective being that of identifying best-practice models. For instance, projects dealt with the comparison of sustainability initiatives in tourist areas; evaluation of the successes and failures surrounding the dissemination of 'sustainable' production methods in agriculture; comparison of the implementation of Agenda 21 (Earth Seminar 7, 1992) at different local levels; comparison of the effects of voluntary or negotiated environmental agreements; or comparison of the efficiency and/or effectiveness of the implementation of European environmental policy or international environmental agreements.

Projects funded under a second sub-area were similar targets. Here the emphasis was on operationalizing information on best practices and producing handbooks, guidelines or inventories, for instance for measuring industrial performance or for involving citizens in 'environment-induced' modernization processes.

While the above two areas were not explicitly defined in policy terms, the work was clearly oriented towards producing policy tools. The third sub-area concentrated on strategic policy development and assessment from the outset. Projects under this heading included studies of the potential impact of environmental change on policy (national and European) or citizen mobilization, and projects for developing so-called 'decision support tools' for bridging theoretical and practical knowledge or for reconceptualizing the planning process in environmental policy formulation. A final set of projects sought to integrate technical assessment into policy analysis.

So far, we have traced the evolution of the EU social environmental research agenda through the details of the work programme's development. From this we have pointed out features that suggest the influence of ecological modernization on the substance of funded research, the expectations from social science, and the framing of 'the environment' and of 'policy relevance' in research. We now turn to a more broad-ranging research policy document in which the ecological modernization project reaches its apotheosis.

Preserving the Ecosystem; Energy, Environment and Sustainable Development, Annex II (European Commission, 1998b) provides 'broad lines of Community activities, scientific and technical objectives'. The preamble reiterates that this programme of research 'will make it possible to meet a wide range of social and economic needs, so reconciling economic development with environmental sustainability'. Sustainable development is then linked to European economic competitiveness (for success in the global market) and social objectives, particularly minimization of unemployment. Scientific research is expected to contribute to this linking process.

The rationale for supporting socio-economic research is also laid out in the claim that 'addressing key societal issues will only be successful if in addition to developing technologies, the socio-economic context is appropriately developed and taken into account' (ibid., p. 2.). Sustainable development has proved difficult to achieve, the document argues, precisely because of deficiencies in 'the tools and methods for formulation and assessment of sustainability policies' (ibid., p. 15). The key to mastering the problem of implementation lies with citizens themselves. The document further decrees that the 'transition to sustainability is based upon consensus and joint action by key stakeholders in a framework of shared responsibility', which in turn demands 'participatory frameworks, so that societal demand can be articulated'.

In other words, the role afforded social science is that of helping to achieve the required 'cultural shifts', without which European policy objectives are expected to remain frustrated. But, even further, social science research is seen as a means of actively *facilitating* policy. This is especially a dominant theme in the recently launched Fifth Framework Programme which states a need for knowledge dissemination and new forms of collaboration between researchers and 'users' or 'stakeholders'. The Fifth Framework seems to illustrate a shift from its predecessor's approach which was largely oriented towards the development of new technologies and policy instruments to a more demand-driven philosophy which claims that consumer and citizen views must be given more attention. Whether this shift will work without contradiction in practice remains to be seen.

National Agendas

The picture emerging from the study of the national research agendas is more nuanced, though broadly similar. Through the late 1970s and early 1980s, research on the environment in most countries was clearly policy-led, with acid rain dominating the research field. Towards the end of the 1980s and in the early 1990s, there was a shift towards cleaner technologies, and socioenvironmental themes began to emerge, albeit not always organized as a distinct agenda. The diffusion of cleaner technologies to small and medium-size companies and more generally of environmental management in the industrial and private sector became a dominant research question. The role of national policy in relation to European environmental policy and the impact of international agreements also came to be frequently addressed in research.

However, there are also interesting exceptions to this trend. Thus the UK's ESRC Global Environmental Change Programme is one of the few to have focused on non-European regional studies, including tropical forests, Sahel Africa and the Arctic region; or the impact of poverty on health in relation to the 'capability' to achieve an environmental quality of life; or the topic of sustainable cities. The last named appears to have become a major theme in the EU's Fifth Framework Programme. In Austria, on the other hand, the research agenda entailed in the 'Cultural Landscapes' Programme has been explicit about the study of conflicts, and the specification of sustainability indicators with particular emphasis on the regional dimension. In both Austria and Finland, transboundary environmental effects and strategies for containing them through regional or bilateral cooperation and technology transfer have likewise been attracting attention as research themes. Given the geographical position of these two countries, this is perhaps not surprising.

Despite the exceptions mentioned above, the drift is still towards social research in support of policy instruments for the introduction of cleaner technologies and for improving efficiency. How is it that EU social environmental research which began with fairly grand theoretical ambitions – such as tackling fundamental relationships between nature and the human, and exploring the sociotechnical pathways towards a sustainable society – should have become so reduced in scope? We take up this question in the next section.

ECOLOGICAL MODERNIZATION AS BOUNDARY OBJECT

In the previous section, we described the way in which multifarious possibilities for social environmental research in the EU have been whittled down to a set of fairly narrow priorities and projects. We have argued that the research agenda was steered in this fashion by the influential discourse of ecological modernization which claims that conflicts between economic growth and competitiveness, environmental sustainability and social benefit can be resolved to the active benefit of all three objectives. Social science is now enrolled as an ally in the implementation of this 'win–win' project. In the process, broad meanings of the environment (as nature), of social science capacity (in terms of contributions arising from various disciplinary perspectives) and of policy-relevant research (imagining generic, even speculative pathways to a sustainable society) seem to have dropped out. Does all this mean that the EU has successfully managed to impose a coherent agenda of its own on the social environmental research community?

In addressing this question, we must first keep in mind that a simple 'imposition' of a coherent project is the wrong way to construct the linkage between research policy makers and researchers, or between the content of environmental policy and social environmental research. As we suggested in opening this chapter, the lines of interaction and influence are far more complex than that, starting with the drafting of work programmes and the development and selection of proposals. The sociological concept of a *boundary object* can be fruitfully applied to explain how research and policy have shaped each other in the social environmental domain.

In scientific work, boundary objects are created when participants from different social worlds collaborate. These objects 'inhabit several intersecting social worlds...*and* satisfy the informational requirements of each of them. ...[they] are both plastic enough to adapt to local needs and the constraints of several parties employing them, yet robust enough to maintain a common identity across sites' (Star and Griesemer, 1989, p. 393). Star and Griesemer develop this concept in the context of their study of a natural history museum in which theorists, sponsors and amateurs collaborated to produce representations of nature. In this case, the boundary objects produced included things like specimens, field notes, maps and the museum itself. The key point to note in their analysis is that each party had their own set of commitments and perceptions; and each of these sets had to be collectively mediated if a joint piece of work was to be produced. In the context of a loosely shared goal, each party worked to achieve their other objectives, creating common objects of reference in the process.

Ecological modernization is both 'plastic' and 'robust' an idea, in that it claims to combine two previously conflicting goals. At its simplest, this means that diverse groups interested in one or the other goal could be brought together in one programme. Thus members of the social research community who were interested in sustainability have effectively reconstructed their research projects to fit within the terms of the ecological modernization agenda. The flexible, yet all-encompassing, nature of ecological modernization means that they have been able to do this while still pursuing their prior interests. The same goes for people interested primarily in issues of economic growth and competitiveness. While some of these people are in mainstream economics, others with a broad interest in political economy or social change, though not 'the environment', also found themselves reconstructing their histories and futures in order to tap into new opportunities. Finally, those researchers who first identified a trend in economic and political reform towards ecological modernization and gave it a name now have an object of study that is becoming embedded in the research policy world and is generating new opportunities for future work.

Turning to EU research managers, we find them engaged in a similar balancing act, juggling between various needs: to develop research to support EU policy and to design a robust research agenda that reflects these policy objectives, to create sufficient demand for social science, and to fund work that has a realistic chance of delivering on its promises. The research that is produced must, in turn, be interpreted in appropriate and coherent terms for other EU stakeholders such as the relevant directorates-general (DGs) and potential users.

Again, given their simultaneous flexibility and robustness, the ideas of ecological modernization enable the management of these conflicting needs.

While ecological modernization aspires to offer integrated, cross-sectoral approaches to the environment, it can be (and has been) conveniently translated into projects that chop up the 'environment' into recognizable and manageable pieces (clean technology, waste, transport and so on) that reflect the already existing interests and commitments of both policy actors and researchers. This does not detract from the fact that the paradigm has managed to stimulate a stream of good and fundable applications. That an all-encompassing framework like ecological modernization seems to have generated research that is rather piecemeal in nature may seem to be a paradox. Our exploration of ecological modernization discourse as a 'boundary object' leads us to conclude that the paradox is not really one at all, insofar as sweeping frameworks may equally well be derived from the convergence of multiple and very specific interests.

In sum, we argue that ecological modernization has served to create and provide with legitimacy a new environmental research and consultancy industry, of which the social sciences are now a part, albeit still at the margins. As the paradigm has expanded from its original focus on the modernization of production to encompass 'sustainable consumption', its core assumptions revolve even more strongly around individual commitment and choice. In the last section of this chapter we offer a critique of ecological modernization as a means of revealing some of the issues and questions that remain to be addressed within its framework.

ECOLOGICAL MODERNIZATION: THE HIDDEN AGENDA

Characteristically absent from the EU's Fourth Framework Programme on the Environment were questions concerning equity or social cohesion. There has been comparatively little research on social inequalities created by global environmental change, on the North–South divide within Europe, on impacts on employment (other than the direct ones relating to job creation from the new environmental industry, especially in the consultancy field), on public acceptability, the willingness but also ability to pay: the real conflicts of interest between economy and ecology or alternatively the barriers to the achievement of the economy–technology–ecology optimum deriving from contradictions inherent in the discourse of ecological modernization.

In seeking greater integration of environmental policy goals with those of other sectors, ecological modernization seeks to accommodate late industrial society. It seeks to redefine international competitiveness in such a way that early technological innovators reap market advantages. It does not represent a threat to capitalist development, and those who argue for ecological modernization do not challenge the logic of international capital. Gouldson and Murphy (1996) note that ecological modernization seems to be rather selective in just where it apportions blame for environmental degradation. It is assumed that advanced industrial societies can shift their technologies and patterns of production while leaving the structures of private capital accumulation fundamentally intact.

There are a number of problems with this approach on the global scale. First, it is insufficiently grounded in international political economy, where recent debates have focused on 'flexible specialization' in production, the primacy of information and associated technology, and internationally differentiated labour markets. Ecological modernization suggests that economic restructuring can be modified to incorporate environmental ends, providing a convergence between productive capital and the environmental goals of society. These 'green' goals serve to act upon the 'real world' of contemporary capitalism, enabling new environmental values to penetrate the very heart of the industrial process. The result is that companies and governments aim to be more competitive in the longer term within the global system. The economic restructuring of global capital is a reality, but in some of the most dynamic economies environmental externalities remain just that, external. In the 'tiger' economies of East Asia, for example, air pollution in cities is growing faster than the rate of economic growth.

As yet, there is little evidence that economic competitiveness has been refashioned to reflect more sustainable objectives. The conviction that ecological modernization represents a way forward for business in no way suggests agreement with higher levels of external regulation, or a commitment to longer-term environmental objectives. Turning the question around, one can equally well ask whether 'labour-saving' ecological modernization strategies can actually produce economic growth – or satisfy the EU's goal of increasing employment – in lagging countries.

Such contradictions are especially severe if we look outside western Europe. The White Paper from the European Commission on Growth, Competitiveness and Employment (1993) states that extrapolating current consumption and production patterns within the European Union to the entire world would require a tenfold increase in resources. Europe's environmental protection industries, the nub of ecological modernization, are currently incapable of shouldering the burden of growth within Europe. It remains to be seen whether 'social coupling', that is, the organization of the workplace around best environmental practice, can work in Germany, Scandinavia or the Netherlands, where it is advocated most strongly. To 'globalize' from European experience would not merely require major shifts in global economies, but would also exacerbate divisions and distributional problems.

Even in the western European context, ecological modernization is still confined to 'end-of-pipe' technologies where environmental regulation is usually operative. It is significant, then, that those who favour environmental regulation usually see ecological modernization as a facet of business development, rather than a means of raising environmental standards. It is argued that business will take ecological modernization seriously once it benefits financially from doing so. Thus a process of accommodation is being favoured, with often generous and flexible time frames for meeting environmental standards. What this has given rise to is a mismatch between the ecological values adhered to by ecological modernization and the technocratic policy packages proposed for putting these principles into practice.

On the whole, ecological modernization does not as yet represent a 'paradigm shift'; it represents rather a trial-and-error process which seeks to obtain a positive-sum interaction between the economy and the environment. This, it should be remembered, has also been the objective of the 'environmental regulation' paradigm. In this the two approaches do not differ. Where they differ is in their preferred mode for achieving this goal: through 'remedy' and the setting of environmental standards in the case of environmental regulation; through 'prevention', and in particular the combination of regulations with economic instruments and a greater emphasis on technological innovation, in the case of ecological modernization.

CONCLUSION

We opened this chapter with the observation that the European social environmental research agenda has progressively converged on a set of priorities related to the implementation of current environmental policies in specific sectors. We then suggested that the discourse of ecological modernization has been at the heart of this trajectory. Following an overview of the project of ecological modernization at the European and national levels, we traced the evolution of the social environmental research agenda and identified the influence of ecological modernist thinking. In seeking to understand how such an apparently coherent agenda had become embedded in the context of European research, we employed the concept of a 'boundary object', and pointed out that both research managers and researchers have found that the core idea of ecological modernization is sufficiently flexible to accommodate their different interests. Finally, we elaborated on a number of tensions entailed by this accommodation between research and research policy, especially those arising from the contradictions and tensions inherent in the ecological modernization concept itself. Especially illustrative is the purported shift from a technology- and policy instrument-driven approach (Fourth Framework Programme) to a demand-driven philosophy that claims to take greater account of citizen and consumer beliefs and needs (Fifth Framework Programme).

In the next chapter, we reflect on our explorations of national research systems (Chapter 2), individual experiences in social environmental research (Chapter 3), and the evolution and flow of research ideas (this chapter) and consider how they might be synthesized in order to capture the overall dynamics of social environmental research networks in Europe.

5. The European dynamics of social environmental research

INTRODUCTION

Since its first research programme under the aegis of EURATOM in 1958, the European Union has steadily taken its research policy to other disciplines and other modes of funding. Especially since its legalisation in 1987 through the Single European Act and the development of structured Framework Programmes, EU research policy has created a niche for itself in European research systems. EU grants for creating networks, transfer of technology, exchange and development of best practices, and mobility schemes for researchers as well as for research projects have made interorganizational collaboration part and parcel of European research practices. In many R&D fields, individual reputations are significantly enhanced through participation in European projects. Research organizations reward European funding obtained by their employees. Governments promote the EU framework programme, take 'Europeanization' to be an important policy theme and take pride in themselves if resources flow back to researchers in their countries.

European research policy has brought about a transformation in both local research practices (through new forms of collaboration) and in national research policies (through a new internationalization). In this context, the way the EU Framework Programme has positioned itself *vis-à-vis* national research policy instruments is of particular interest. In 1983, the 'Reisenhuber criteria' were formulated to create a space for European action. These criteria state that the involvement of the then European Community in funding research is legitimate in the following cases:

- research conducted on so vast a scale that single member states could not, or could not without difficulty, provide sufficient financial means and personnel;
- research which would obviously benefit financially from being carried out jointly, after taking account of the additional costs of international collaboration;

- research which would achieve significant results in the whole of the Community for problems on the international scale, owing to the complementary nature of national efforts;
- research which contributes to the cohesion of the common market and which promotes the unification of European science and technology, as well as research which leads where necessary to the establishment of uniform laws and standards.

Within these criteria one can distinguish the two principles of the Framework Programme: *subsidiarity* and *unification*. The principle of subsidiarity implies that the EU should leave to the nation states what they do best, and only take responsibility if there is a European 'added value' (Guzzetti, 1995). The other principle is that the Frameworks Programme should improve competitiveness and cohesion through unification.

In the context of relationships between the EU and national research systems, there is clearly a tension between these two principles. The subsidiarity principle assumes a vertical relationship between the EU and nation states, and identifies the EU as a supranational body. It stresses differences in responsibilities between the EU and the nation states, akin to those in federal states between federal and regional governments. The ambitions of competitiveness and cohesion, on the contrary, stress the horizontal relationships that span the boundaries of national research systems. Here the Community is not a body above the member states, but a force for unification that might be expected to produce a denationalization of research systems. How the Framework Programme affects national research systems in general, and national capacities for social environmental research in particular, can only be understood by looking more closely into the dynamics of the programme itself. In this chapter, we explore the extent to which the SEER and Human Dimensions programmes have added a new, supranational level to European social environmental research systems, as opposed to merging them into one system. In order to address this question, we first need to understand the international context within which these EU-funded programmes themselves exist.

The EU is not the only international player in the field of social environmental research, nor do its programmes represent the only mechanism for transnational scientific cooperation. Though their motivations vary, other agencies are equally committed to international collaboration, the sharing of ideas and expertise, and the pooling of intellectual and financial resources. As a result, international scientific collaboration within Europe does not take place within a monolithic structure but is instead distributed across a web of organizations, programmes and initiatives. In the field of social environmental research, key points in this web include the International Human Dimensions Programme (IHDP), the European Science Foundation's Programme on

Tackling Environmental Resource Management (ESF-TERM) and the Greening of Industry Network (GIN). We therefore begin this chapter with a rather straightforward analysis of the Environment and Climate programme of the EU and its Human Dimensions research theme in juxtaposition with these other international initiatives in the area of social environmental research.

Having studied in earlier chapters the dynamics of national structures, of researcher strategies and of the EU research agenda, the juxtaposition of these different international programmes suggests that European social environmental research may be conceptualized as a *network of networks*. This concept blurs the boundaries between national and international research programmes and systems, on the one hand, and allows for the creation of distinct and concentrated nodes of influence within the field of social environmental research, on the other. In order to capture the dynamics by which such a network of networks develops and functions, we analyse the machinery of the Framework Programme later in this chapter. As researchers respond to the programmes and research projects develop, the practices and processes of this machinery extend beyond Brussels. Through these research strategies and project lives, the EU programme becomes linked to the research programmes of other environmental institutes, national research bodies and international agencies. The chapter concludes by examining the general implications of the 'network of networks' concept for locating the EU SEER and Human Dimensions programmes in the wider world of social environmental research.

EU SOCIAL ENVIRONMENTAL RESEARCH IN INTERNATIONAL CONTEXT

Science has long been an international activity. Indeed, the very notion of a 'scientific community' tends to signify that scientists belong to a group whose interests and methods of enquiry transcend national boundaries. Nevertheless, the internationalization of science, in the sense of the density of formal research linkages between actors in different countries, is a fairly recent phenomenon. Witnessed since the 1950s, this process has further intensified since the 1980s when the growing scale of human and financial resources required for science and technology obliged government and research bodies to cooperate at the international level (OECD, 1991).

The international dimensions of the environment-and-climate problem, and of the policies developed in response to it, would seem to demand international collaboration in research conducted on the subject. Such collaboration has taken the form of a profusion of international initiatives, agreements, collaborations and programmes oriented towards research. The first initiatives were made around 1970 when the International Council of Scientific Unions (ICSU) established the Scientific Committee on Problems of the Environment (SCOPE), while UNESCO established its Man and the Biosphere (MAB) programme. With the emergence of the idea of global change in the 1980s, ICSU developed the International Geosphere–Biosphere Programme (IGBP). Since then, many other international organizations and agencies have become involved, either under the umbrella of the IGBP or with their own initiatives (Price, 1990). Indeed, in 1996, the Dutch advisory council on Nature and Environmental research (RMNO) found 50 such international programmes and 350 national programmes in 13 European countries (RMNO, 1996). The council also identified a total of 121 international networks in which Dutch researchers claimed to participate in the field of human dimensions of global environmental change (RMNO, 1994; see also special issue of *The Globe*, 1997).

Environment and climate research shows internationalization not only at the level of formal research programmes, but also in research content, especially around models of environmental systems and climate change (Kwa, 1993). Through international programmes like the IGBP that try to orchestrate activities and funding, climate change research has come to be institutionalized around the notion of *system* (Jasanoff and Wynne, 1998). This internationalization of environmental and climate research has led to the formation of what may be called *research regimes*. Borrowed from regime theory in the study of international relations (Krasner, 1983; Young, 1989), the notion of 'research regimes' refers to the intrinsically international networks of activity in various fields of enquiry. Such networks lack explicit centralized nodes of control and consist of a multiplicity of sub-systems and sub-regimes, yet they often exhibit an apparently common purpose and a shared set of world-views or questions. Unlike international collaboration in, for instance, high energy physics, the research regime in environmental and climate research shows internationalization also at the level of interaction between researchers and policy makers within specific epistemic communities (Haas, 1989; 1992).

Given the domination of systems thinking and computer modelling in the international environment and climate research regime, the conditions for social environmental research may not seem particularly favourable (Redclift and Benton, 1994). The EU's SEER and Human Dimensions of Environment and Climate programmes chronicled in this book attest to the fact that the social sciences have created a space for themselves in this research regime. The other international initiatives described in this chapter – IHDP, the GIN initiative and the ESF-TERM programme – provide additional evidence of social science activity. Like the EU programmes, these initiatives aim to stimulate and improve social research on the environment by promoting and coordinating research activities under specific themes. Implicitly or explicitly, they seek to stimulate the exchange of ideas and the development of new thinking via the creation of networks. However, they differ in their organizational structure, flow of funding and articulation of their respective agendas.

We begin mapping the international context of EU social environmental research by providing brief overviews of each of the initiatives in this field. In these descriptions, we deliberately stay as close as possible to the original texts and formal descriptions of the programmes, leaving comparison, contrast and critical analyses to later sections of the chapter.

The EU Environment and Climate Programme

The formal organizational features and origins of the EU's programmes have already been described at length in Chapter 1. Here we provide a brief synopsis that sets the stage for comparison with other international initiatives. The first phase of social environmental research in the EU began within the Third Framework Programme (1990–94) under the label of Socio-Economic Environmental Research (SEER). A total of 120 projects involving over 400 individual researchers were funded under SEER. An informal review stated that, although the programme was relatively minor in size and budget within the Framework Programmes, it was the most comprehensive effort of socio-economic environmental research in the Community, and that 'this modest investment has helped to trigger a significant research effort in both theory and in policy analysis in human dimensions of environmental change' (European Commission, 1998c).

In the Fourth Framework Programme, research on the global environment was structured within a programme on Environment and Climate (1994–98) which eventually funded a total of 89 projects. The objectives of the programme were as follows:

- to better understand the processes underlying environmental change, in particular those of the climate system, including the atmosphere, the oceans, the land surfaces, the continental ice masses and the biosphere;
- to improve assessment of the consequences of climatic and other environmental change;
- to contribute to the identification, formulation and implementation of societal policy and technological responses to global environmental change;
- to contribute to the technological development necessary for environmental observation, monitoring and research, including methodologies and technologies for the monitoring, warning and management of natural hazards. (European Commission, 1996).

A total budget of 526 million ECU was split across four themes (see Table 5.1). Social environmental research was organized within the theme of Human

Dimensions of Environmental Change, with 7.5 per cent of the total budget. Aiming to 'improve the basis of policies and actions in support of sustainable development in the EU', the work programme for this theme specified the following four areas:

- socioeconomic causes and effects of environmental change,
- economic and societal responses to environmental problems – towards sustainable development,
- integration of scientific knowledge, economic and societal considerations into the formulation of environmental policies,
- sustainable development and technological change.

Table 5.1   EU Environment and Climate Programme, 1994–8

Theme	Budget (m.ECU)
1 Research into the natural environment, environmental quality and global change	247.75 (47.1%)
2 Environmental technologies	131.25 (25%)
3 Space techniques applied to environmental monitoring and research	107.60 (20.5%)
4 Human dimensions of environmental change	39.40 (7.5%)
Total	526 (100.1%)

The programme staff located at DGXII of the European Commission in Brussels were responsible for managing the formulation of the work programme, calls for tenders, contract negotiations and evaluations. Each project was assigned a Commission staff officer who was expected to oversee progress and function as a link between project team and the Commission. Calls were issued for research project proposals in accordance with the general procedures of the framework programmes which laid out the Commission's evaluation criteria and format for submissions. Proposals were assessed by independent evaluators in two rounds that considered their scientific and technical quality, and their strategic, economic and policy relevance, respectively. Evaluators were given detailed instructions on the criteria for assessment and their relative weight. Ultimately, decisions for funding were made by the Commission.

The International Human Dimensions Programme (IHDP)

Originally launched in 1990 as the Human Dimensions Programme by the International Social Sciences Council (ISSC) with seven priority topics, the

IHDP is an interdisciplinary, non-governmental programme dedicated to the promotion and coordination of research rather than the funding of specific projects. With ICSU joining ISSC in 1996 as co-sponsor, IHDP was restructured to concentrate on fewer topics related to the human dimensions of global environmental change and to aim at the delivery of timely and visible results. Seen as a test case for cooperation between the natural and the social sciences, it aims to build upon existing research by expanding and strengthening international networks of communication in this area. Specifically, the IHDP seeks to:

- bring together researchers, policy makers and other stakeholders in the international arena,
- generate synergies between different national and regional research committees and programmes,
- gather and structure existing research into broader themes,
- identify new research priorities and
- facilitate dissemination of research results.

These goals are directed towards the understanding of the ways in which individuals and societies contribute to, are influenced by, and mitigate and adapt to global environmental change. In this, the IHDP outlines its motivations in terms of the fact that global environmental change has become both a highly visible scientific issue and one that has evoked increasing pressure for the adoption of appropriate policies. This, in turn, has sparked new demands for the generation of reliable information from research communities. IHDP therefore strives for collaboration between its own network and its three partner programmes also sponsored by the ISCU and the ISSC in the environmental field: the World Climate Research Programme (WCRP), the International Geosphere–Biosphere Programme (IGBP) and the International Programme of Biodiversity Science (DIVERSITAS). Along with WCRP and IGBP, the IHDP sponsors a System for Analysis, Research and Training (START) whose networking mission focuses particularly on the regional level.

The visibility of environmental change as a global issue has come to require an explicitly international pooling of efforts that encompasses developing countries as well as advanced industrial nations. To this end, the IHDP has enrolled over 20 national committees of scientists working on human dimensions, helping in the establishment of some and fortifying the work of others. Its scientific committee also comprises scientists from different national and disciplinary backgrounds. All activities are coordinated by the Secretariat located, since 1996, in Bonn. The IHDP supports four science projects at present:

1. *Land-Use and Land-Cover Change (LUCC)* The role of land use and land cover in global environmental change has been widely recognized in envi-

ronmental research and environmental policy. LUCC is a joint research initiative of IHDP and the IGBP, which calls for a set of integrative research foci and activities in an effort to improve understanding of: (a) the driving forces (exogenous variables) of land use as they operate through the land manager; (b) the land-cover implications of land use; (c) the spatial and temporal variability in land-use/cover dynamics; and (d) regional and global models and projections of land-use/cover change (Turner *et al.*, 1995).

2. *Global Environmental Change and Human Security (GECHS)*   This is a research project focusing on the interrelationships between environmental change, resource use, vulnerability and conflict. It aims to provide additional empirical studies on environmental change and its relationship to a broader conception of security as well as to improve communication among researchers, policy makers and NGOs (Lonergan *et al.*, 1999).

3. *Institutional Dimensions of Global Change (IDGC)*   This project analyses the roles that social institutions play as determinants of the course of human–environment interactions. It is based on the observation that institutions loom large as causes of large-scale environmental problems that are both systemic (for example, climate change, ozone layer depletion) and cumulative (for example, loss of biological diversity) in nature. Conversely, institutions often figure prominently in efforts to solve or manage environmental problems (Young 1999).

4. *Industrial Transformation (IT)*   The research agenda of this project focuses on the relationship between changes in the industrial systems and changes in the environment. Based on the assumption that production and consumption systems have to be changed in order to be able to meet needs of a growing world population, its objective is to discover ways to decrease the environmental impacts of industrial activities (Vellinga, 1999).

These projects, just like the IHDP itself, function mostly as an agenda. If individual scientists or institutes are interested in a project, they can use the IHDP label and IHDP contacts to work within it. Project agendas are therefore initiated by a small group of people who put forth their ideas in the form of a science plan which then becomes the subject of brainstorming at international workshops before a research programme is eventually orchestrated. Participants raise their own funds with the assistance of the IHDP secretariat and committees.

Following the 1997 meeting of the IHDP Scientific Committee, a new two-track work programme was endorsed. In conjunction with the four projects already in place, new priorities and topics were to be identified and placed in a second track of work. Together, an overall Science Plan would be put in place. Initial thoughts on overarching themes were laid out by invitation by two members of the committee at this meeting and the next. Potential topics included health and the environment, urbanization, individual roles in global environmental change and integration of human dimension aspects into climate change models.

The Greening of Industry Network (GIN)

Founded by Johan Schot (the Netherlands) and Kurt Fischer (USA) with a planned 10-year lifetime, GIN aims to be a very open, informal network, focusing on the exchange of ideas and information in the area of industry responses to and management of environmental concerns. Led by social scientists, it places a great deal of emphasis on participation by potential research users in industry, government and NGOs, as well as anyone, regardless of status, who has something relevant and interesting to contribute. GIN has its origins in a 1989 study tour that Schot – senior researcher at the time at the Dutch TNO Centre for Technology and Policy Studies – undertook of the USA to learn about the then new and fragmented area of environmental management. Hooking up with Fischer at the Center for Environmental Management (Tufts University) who was developing strategies for coordination of environmental research, education, policy and outreach, Schot became convinced that research should develop in interaction with users. The two devised plans to set up an international network on the Greening of Industry, whose first formal activities included annual research conferences, publication of a book series and the establishment of cooperation with the journal, *Business Strategy and the Environment.*

Discussions among 70 invited participants at the first conference in 1991 revealed a general consensus on the need for a research network in this area. They felt that there is a need to know how and why companies behave the way they do in affecting the environment; this knowledge could help improve existing policies and generate new ways of changing company behaviour. Subsequently, GIN's mission was formulated as follows:

- to promote the creation, conduct and dissemination of theoretically informed empirical research on the greening of industry,
- to connect researchers and research organizations across disciplines and internationally, and
- to influence research agenda setting and policy development

An international advisory board with members from different countries and backgrounds was also set up with branches in Europe and the USA. By the time of the next conferences, in 1993 and 1995, GIN managed to bring in a handful of participants from developing countries. Workshops have also been held on more structured themes. The network's mission and goals were re-examined along the way, and issues of urgent strategic importance identified, including increasing the involvement of business and NGOs, and organizing a conscious process of action-research agenda building. In 1995, through various workshops and interviews, the content of GIN's research agenda was also narrowed down to focus on four main themes: (a) integrated strategies for transformation towards sustainable development, (b) changing consumption patterns, (c) finance capital and performance indicators, and (d) technological breakthroughs (Schot *et al.*, 1997).

A further step towards agenda building was the establishment of a link between GIN through European and American coordinators, Theo de Bruijn and David Angel, and the IHDP's project on Industrial Transformation (IT) which is coordinated by Pier Vellinga (Free University, Amsterdam). GIN members eventually came to serve on IHDP's Scientific Planning Committee. Latest developments include the setting up of an Asian network node in Bangkok.

Apart from some administrative support provided in its first three years, GIN raises its own funds for each activity. Personal contacts with European Union and national research managers can be important in this regard, as for example, between Schot and Sors, head of the EU climate research programme. Despite problems of continuity in funding created by the explicit rejection of institutionalization, the network itself has managed to expand and sustain itself through informal links. A question for the future is whether GIN should continue at all in its present form or find an institutional link from which to influence policy.

European Science Foundation's (ESF) Programme on Tackling Environmental Resource Management (TERM)

The TERM programme grew out of a decision taken in 1994 by the ESF Standing Committee for the Social Sciences to allocate unspent money from the Environment, Science and Society Programme to new activities. In the process, social science research on the environment was reinforced as a high-priority strategic area. A planning group consisting of northern European members with previous experience in this area was set up, and the ground prepared for a new social science activity under the title of 'Tackling Environmental Resource Management' (TERM).

As a pioneer of social research on the environment, the Environment, Science and Society Programme had helped establish an interdisciplinary network of researchers and influenced subsequent European initiatives such as the EU's own SEER, as well as major international conferences in the field. TERM was envisaged as a way of building on these achievements. Proposed as an umbrella theme to include the range of topics covered by national programmes, TERM was intended to provide a forum for debate and exchange of communication between researchers. In this, its objective was specifically that of coordinating and focusing at a European level the institutionally fragmented experiences and findings from partner countries.

A major aim was to pool expertise from national projects by providing a 'breathing-space' for researchers to reflect on medium- and long-term needs. The planners recognized early on that national programmes were either in different stages of development or simply did not exist as such in some countries, being found rather in various government departments, research councils or private organizations. National research was metaphorically described as being fraught with 'butterfly-catcher syndrome' – research often having a national focus (the 'net') and concentrating on a specific topic (the 'butterfly') – hence calling for comparative efforts. The fact that a substantial amount of social environmental research work was done on a short-term contract basis was also noted. This called for the pooling of resources, not only for scientific purposes, but also in order to address training and career development issues in a field in which interdisciplinarity was crucial. These objectives were to be tackled through support for workshops, summer schools, exchange of doctoral students and debates with invited policy makers.

While not limited to European topics, the research themes were to reflect existing European capacity. Following the first consultative workshop in 1995, the following themes which have continued into the second phase of TERM (1998 onwards) were identified:

1. comparative dynamics of consumption and production processes,
2. policy-oriented learning and decision making: environmental management and policy instruments under uncertainty,
3. forms of international environmental cooperation and their development,
4. perception, communication and the social representation of environmental change.

From early on in its history, TERM has explicitly aimed to avoid overlap with other major international efforts in social environmental research such as the IHDP and those of the EU. For the first workshop, the planning group delib-erately decided against inviting observers from these other programmes. This was motivated by the desire to first take stock of existing *national* efforts and achievements and set out priorities for cross-fertilization before deciding on how best to coordinate TERM with other international activities. Since then, col-laboration with the National Science Foundation (USA) and the EU's DGXII and co-sponsorship of some activities have taken place.

FOUR PROGRAMMES AND A NETWORK

The above descriptions make it clear that social environmental research is carried out within a number of international programmes. To understand the role of the

EU within this international research regime, it is useful to compare and contrast the ambitions, agendas and management structures of the different bodies.

As we have already pointed out, the EU's Human Dimensions programme operated according to a strict set of procedures, and within a clear political framework. While its budget was negligible in the context of the Framework Programme, it may have looked like a bonanza in relation to some other areas of research. The TERM programme has some funding at its disposal, but only to finance workshops, exchanges and summer schools. On the other hand, both the IHDP and the GIN initiatives depend on the ability of coordinators and project leaders to raise funds. They live on resource opportunities provided by national and international programmes, research institutions and environmental policy agencies.

The EU programme also differs from the other initiatives in terms of the role that individual researchers are accorded. Like the other programmes, the EU depends on the participation of researchers for the development of a research programme as well as the selection of proposals. However, in the actual doing of research, researchers function solely as contractors. By contrast, the IHDP and TERM programmes delegate management responsibility to the offices of researchers, whereas management is distributed over three coordinating centres in the case of the GIN. The delegation of management not only acts to put the parent organizations and temporary participants at a distance, but also gives researchers the responsibility for developing social environmental research. Further, some researchers in these programmes also reach out to the policy world and, to some extent, help define the policy context. In the EU, by contrast, the policy framework is already established by the programme.

Such differences in management practice are all too easily equated with a difference in 'top-down' and 'bottom-up' management, as if policy makers are always at the top in research systems and researchers at the bottom. Such a perspective is hardly tenable within the international environmental research regime. If there is a difference in governance style within the functioning of the programme it is to be found in the ambitions of coordination and control displayed by each of the programmes. The EU's Human Dimensions programme represents an attempt to coordinate social environment research through a focused policy-led agenda and to control activities by using strict selection procedures and research contracts. While the IHDP has similar ambitions, it lacks the financial resources to translate them into research funds and contracts. Instead, it mobilizes the scientific reputation of key figures within international environmental research, committing them to the ambitions of IHDP through membership of national committees and the joint authorship of scientific plans. In return, its linkages with IGBP, WCRP and DIVERSITAS offer the prestige of becoming involved in an international research regime with the concomitant opportunities to use the IHDP label to raise more funds.

In this respect, GIN was more modest at the start, being an informal network for exchange of ideas between researchers and users. Over time and in the aftermath of successful initiatives, the position of the network became stronger and more defined. The development of a research agenda and the linkage with the IHDP Industrial Transformation project demonstrate this stronger position and reveal the ambition to use that position to play a key role in research on ecological modernization of industry.

The span of control the programmes aim for is reflected in the scope of their agendas. The Human Dimensions and, especially, the IHDP programme include a broad area of research issues in their agenda. The GIN and TERM programmes concentrate on more specific issues. All four programmes share a commitment to the ambitions of improving knowledge in the social environmental research and putting it to use for environmental and climate policies. More specifically, they have framed their agendas around an increasingly dominant interpretation of the environmental problem and of sustainable development. The subject areas of 'environmental technology', 'industrial technology', 'greening of industry' and 'environmental resource management' are all part of the wider agenda of ecological modernization by which, as was described in Chapter 4, sustainable development has been defined in terms of mutually beneficial inter-actions between economy, technology and the environment.

A Network of Networks

The existence of a broadly common research agenda suggests that several linkages between the different initiatives might exist. Formal connections between IHDP and GIN, collaboration between TERM and the EU's Fifth Framework environmental programme, and funding for several GIN activities that existed under the EU's Human Dimensions programme are only some instances of such overlap. Looking at who is active within these programmes, for instance serving on the scientific committee or at the planning workshops, or simply coordinating a project, we find linkages between the different initiatives to be even more close. Returning to our concept of 'serial operators' (Chapter 3), we note that there is a loose cohort of individuals who occupy multiple roles in the European social environmental research field, acting as research suppliers, advisors, experts and managers in a variety of related inter-national contexts. Acting as they do to connect people and ideas in these different institutional research settings, these serial operators may be seen as the builders of the European 'network of networks'.

Since TERM, IHDP and GIN do not commission or fund research of their own, they depend on the existence of other funding bodies, either national or the EU, to support and fuel the researchers on whom they depend and whom they seek to connect. Therefore another way of identifying the creation of the 'network of networks' is to examine programme descriptions and structures for the flow of funds. Thus, for example, we see that the ESF receives financial support from national governments and research councils that have their own environmental programmes as well. We see that the 1996 establishment of the IHDP secretariat in Bonn was partly financed by the University of Bonn, as well as the German, Dutch, Norwegian and American governments. The founding conference of the GIN received financial support from nine European and American organizations, ranging from the EU's DGXII to Dutch and American government departments and universities, as well as some international science-based associations.

The interdependency between different initiatives has created a system of money, ideas and researchers circulating at a specifically *European* level, which is hardly the sum total of distinct international programmes, or a level distinct from national levels. As a consequence, it makes no sense to talk about the EU's Human Dimensions programme as a monolithic structure with clearly defined boundaries demarcating, for example, a European research community or research agenda subsidiary to national communities and agendas. Instead, the programme is shown to be a node – albeit a very important one – amongst other nodes in a much broader, sprawling web of interconnections which represent European social environmental research. The picture that emerges from the above is one of an international space or landscape within a web of multiple networks that are connected to each other in a number of ways (Vinck *et al.*, 1993). We see a network of networks, an image which Figure 5.1 captures on a (too limited) two-dimensional scale.

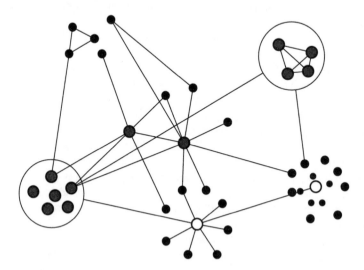

Figure 5.1   'Networks and networks' – multiple networks in a (three) dimensional research landscape

The little circles in this figure could represent localized activities of social environmental research, either in the form of a project, the current research activity of a research group or management of a research programme or network. Some of such localized activities are held together at the 'national level' (Chapter 2) within a research institute or department, or roughly in the same geographical location. Some national systems are not really systems at all, in that they basically consist of a smattering of isolated researchers located across the country: the large circle at the bottom, left-hand corner with its little individual dots represents a fragmented system of this kind (such as in Spain). Alternatively, the figure to its right shows a central node to which other nodes are connected; this suggests a system with a centralized research programme (such as in the UK). Other localized activities are connected with what we identify as international programmes and networks, standing out in crossing national geographic boundaries, but being similar in the sense of being connected with a set of other localized activities.

Within this web, researchers navigate their way between different nodes that may include their national research systems, but might simply be an independent European or international node. Their activities therefore give rise to 'epistemic communities' whose membership transcends both national and organizational/programme boundaries (Haas, 1992). As far as research agendas are concerned, these exist as boundary objects, swimming across the intersecting nodes of the network of networks, and aligning them by satisfying the disparate demands of each (Star and Griesemer, 1989).

EUROPEAN DYNAMICS OF SOCIAL ENVIRONMENTAL RESEARCH

In constructing the above map of European social environmental research, we are still faced with the problem that, like the spatial conceptualization in national and European levels of research, the conceptualization in a network space is a static one. In order to understand the dynamics and flows of our network of networks, we analyse the development of three entities within different time–space configurations. First, we look at the machinery of the Human Dimensions programme and how the programme's identity evolves as it moves from the offices in Brussels to research institutes in Europe. Second, we look at a few hours in the fictional diary of a prototypical 'serial operator' to see how, within only a short time span, linkages are created between past and future projects and between research activities distributed over Europe. Third, we follow the life of a project, again a fictional one, to see how researchers find each other, and how they pursue divergent interests within the shared project space.

The Machinery of the Framework Programme

Funding bodies and research programmes often employ standardized processes which, like machines, attempt to process and give appreciable shape to a diversity of ingredients by means of a structured set of hardware transformed into products that are standardized in some predefined fashion (Rip, 1999). The hardware of the machine includes a parent organization, financial resources, a staff complement (programme managers, secretariat and so on), a programme and/or advisory committee, an official call for proposals, and so on. The processing of ingredients, that is, a variety of people with different backgrounds, and ideas in a range of forms, takes place through a series of (virtually automated) steps which connect various elements of the hardware. Typically, such processes involve holding consultative founding workshops, tendering for and selecting proposals and, ultimately, evaluating the programme itself. As a result, over time, what is signified as the 'content' of the programme is produced: that is, the work programme, the research projects and research results, and all that is between. Such formal activities in each of the programme machines also leave material traces in the shape of documents (calls for proposals, meeting minutes, reports) and databases (of projects, individuals, measured outcomes). These also count as outputs in that they are used in various ways by the actors to articulate what the programme is about.

Implicit in the bare bones of our description of the EU programming machine is the idea that linkages exist with a myriad of actors and processes – formal and informal, public and private – that fall outside the machine itself. A founding workshop will, for example, involve key stakeholders from outside the DGXII bureaucracy, some of whom might end up sitting on a programme or advisory committee. Of these linkages, the most crucial involves researchers, without whom the machine simply cannot operate. Otherwise, the programme machine is simply a text or script that spells out programme ambitions, with staff and earmarked funding. Clearly, the programme is reliant on researchers and, hence, the logic of the machine requires a tendering process. This point may well seem self-evident, and thus not worth stressing. However, the solicitation of programme participants induces two intricately linked processes that are crucial to an understanding of the way EU programmes work: the establishment of transnational project teams, and the (re)definition of the programme's content or agenda.

Since transnational collaboration is a condition of EU funding, the tendering process sets in motion a process whereby individual researchers search across countries for collaborators willing and able to form a project team (Chapter 3). Whatever the individual incentives for participating in EU projects, our research shows that partners tend to bring with them priorities that reflect their own national or local experiences and interests. Here we see the first indication of a fundamental tension between programme-level ambitions and the substantive interests of programme participants. At a project level, it is the task of project coordinators to address this tension by pulling partners towards a common European goal, preventing them from focusing too strongly on their own national or local priorities. The results of these efforts are reflected in the content of actual proposals submitted to the programme. In selecting projects from the range of proposals submitted, programme managers also confront the tensions inherent in programming: they have European priorities to realize, yet need to enlist participants, which means having to cater to their local or national interests.

Both the writing of research proposals by project participants and the selection of projects by programme managers involve a (re)negotiation and (re)shaping of the original programme agenda. For example, the agency specifies the sorts of activities eligible for funding in its call for proposals. The document aims to balance the competing demands of knowledge production (in quantitative terms) and coherence by bounding the range of potentially relevant projects by means of a set of themes and headings. In preparing a response, potential collaborators will try to work with and around this official programme. They need to balance the demands of viability against the range of frequently different expectations, interests and backgrounds that each of them bring to the planned project. If the project being planned is an extended workshop of the type funded by the ESF, the range of issues that need to be winnowed down and given shape to is even more extensive than in the course of the average research project.

At the end of this process of negotiation, the final proposal may look significantly different from the original expectations of the funders, to the extent that such expectations were clearly developed in the first place. Part of this twisting out of a workable project from the sweeping plan produced by the programme machine is simply the normal translation of generic objectives into specific themes: for instance, from the funder's interest in 'the evolution of society's relations with the environment, its industrial and social metabolism' to the researchers' projects on pressure-cookers and fridge-freezers, transport choices, car pooling and so on. The Human Dimensions programme agenda for developing indicators of sustainable development, evaluating policy instruments and providing up-to-date intelligence about people's environmental values implies that social science is expected to have a significant, but remarkably narrow, role with respect to natural science and environmental policy. In practice, the range of projects funded addressed a wider range of questions and included studies which were explicitly critical of this view of social science, as well as those which conformed to it.

The content of EU research programmes thus changes as its internal dynamics unfold: from the call for proposals, a text which defines key priorities, to a set of submitted proposals, to the subsequent selection of projects. During this process, the underlying tensions between (European) programme-level ambitions and (national or local) individual interests play themselves out as mutual flows of influence between the programme and its participants. In very basic terms, the programme determines the profile of its pool of participants, and the latter give content to the programme itself. The process of giving content inevitably takes shape as a *'projectization'*, a strength in terms of the capacity to provide focus, and a weakness in terms of the creation of gaps or the avoidance of environmentally relevant issues that do not fit neatly into a project package. In any case, 'projectization' means not only that research is carried out in the form of multiple projects at any point in the life of a programme, but also that a *chain* of projects is set in motion. This then implies a flow (and the repackaging) of people and ideas through the European double market, a point we attempt to capture through the following fictional accounts of a day in the life of a serial operator, and of the life of a typical research project.

The Diary of a Serial Operator

Rob is the director of a social sciences research and training institute, and chairman of one of the national IHDP committees. This committee has close ties with the national advisory committee on environmental policy and the national social science research council, as well as a research programme on climate change. In addition, Rob was involved in the founding workshops of the EU's SEER programme, as well as the ESF's TERM programme, apart from being a partner in an EU SEER project that is nearing completion. His networking activities within the field of social environmental research also include acting as an expert reviewer of projects or programmes, contributing to workshops, doing the conference circuit, and so on.

29 May 1999
Rob got in early this morning, dreading the stack of post and e-mail and voice messages that must surely have piled up over the past week. Still, he tells himself, the conference in Helsinki was better than he had expected. He even managed to get people in some boring sessions talking about 'nature' and why social scientists have got to talk about it! Sure enough, his pigeonhole is overflowing and the red light on his phone is flashing away madly. He avoids thinking about turning on the computer for the present.

As he sorts through his post, he is glad to toss a pile of 'junk' into the bin. He stops, noticing a letter from Rebecca in London. She says that she is organizing a workshop on 11 September on 'Emissions trading instruments', and invites Rob to attend. Rob is at first disinclined, telling himself that he just did one such workshop six months back. Also Rebecca's workshop is to be right after a two-day holiday that he plans to snatch after a meeting in Toulouse on the ninth connected with the SEER project. This would leave him in the position of spending a day in London after the flight back from France doing nothing. Just as he is about to put the letter aside, he asks himself, who else is going to be there? He notes without interest the names of people he has been seeing rather frequently at meetings on related topics. On the other hand, the prospect of meeting Fred, whom he has not seen since last year's meeting in Prague, does seem attractive. Rob vacillates for a moment and moves on to his e-mail.

Not surprisingly, he finds 144 new messages awaiting him. The delete key serves him well on more than a few occasions. After he forwards an invitation to attend the next meeting of IHDP to a colleague, he finds the second draft of a Fifth Framework proposal on ecological modernization that is currently in the works. Sheila, the coordinator, needs to find a partner in Portugal; Rob suggests Teresa whom he met at a TERM workshop.

As he scrolls down, Rob comes across an e-mail from Watson mentioning, among other things, that Fred – who will be at the London workshop – is now with the OECD. Rob begins to find Rebecca's invitation more than mildly interesting. He knows that it would be good to catch up with Fred and get the inside scoop on this new research programme on environment and economy. On second thoughts, he could also avoid wasting a day in London after his holiday, by trying to arrange an interview with the Royal Institute of International Affairs on the tenth. His mind is made up, and he dashes off a note indicating that he would be happy to attend.

As Rob prints his letter, he hears one of his research assistants, Samantha, coming in. He hopes that she has sorted out all the people for their Framework proposal on biodiversity. It needs to be put together by 7 June at least in order to make the 15 June deadline. Rob also recalls that Samantha was supposed to be setting up interviews with the Department of the Environment, Transport and the Regions (DETR) on their ESRC project on environmental economics.

Samantha comes in, looking somewhat dejected. She immediately plunges into the bad news that Maria from Spain and Jan from the Netherlands both need to be struck off the list of potential partners for their Framework proposal. Jan has said no; Maria has yet to respond to several e-mails. Also, on the DETR interviews, Samantha says that she tried to convince Neil to give them an interview: she gave him the story about Rob's previous involvement in regional planning, and said they would like to meet him to talk about the 4.4 million homes issue. But Neil wouldn't have any of it – he said he did remember Rob, but what they have to say is all in the documents and he didn't see the need for a meeting.

Rob tries to calm his assistant down and offers a few suggestions. Samantha asks if he has read her PhD proposal; Rob apologizes, saying that he did not get around to it. The phone rings at that point – it's Barbara from the university finance office, who says that, since sterling has dropped considerably against the ECU, the centre may not have enough to pay researcher Eric's salary for the last two months. Rob asks for the figures.

Rob returns to the rest of his e-mail, hoping that things will improve. He sees that Anna wants him to be involved in a framework bid for a European network for exchange and dissemination of research on ecological modernization – the deadline is barely two weeks away! He phones Anna immediately and says yes, knowing that this is a good opportunity for future generation of research income. Anna does not have any contacts in Greece, and asks if Rob could suggest someone. Rob pulls out his file from the previous year's HOMER project and suggest Carlos. He then asks about the part of the end-of-award report that Anna and her assistant were supposed to be writing for the ESF workshop. Anna wants until next week to do it, Rob says that he is off to Amsterdam on Monday for an IHDP committee meeting and must send off the final report by then. The tone seems to have been set for the rest of the day.

The international context of EU social environmental research is particularly vivid in this fictional diary. The fact that Rob was involved in the setting up of both SEER and TERM programmes, apart from having a foot in the IHDP, illustrates one way in which these international programmes are interwoven. By moving across different initiatives, certain key individuals make the links and literally create a network in social environmental research that extends beyond the EU alone. These links in turn enable one programme to draw from the pool of expertise of another: for example, Rob is able to draw from the contacts made at a TERM meeting to suggest a potential Portuguese partner for a SEER proposal. However, the cross-cutting of initiatives can also pose problems insofar as the same few individuals are called upon for participation in workshops or new proposals; limitations on any one person's time mean that some of these invitations may be successfully delegated, while others fall by the wayside. Delegation of tasks can create its own troubles: thus Rob's research assistant who lacks his cultural capital is unable to set up a research interview with a key official.

This exercise in sketching a typical social environmental research serial operator's working day allows us to illustrate three central points about the functioning of the European machine. One is that many of these linkages are constructed outside the formal confines of the EU world; thus the EU machine sets in motion processes out of its own control. Yet these subsequent activities are absolutely central to the functioning of the research system. Secondly, programme participants (and hence, programmes) connect up in an incredible variety of settings, many of which take place simultaneously. The multiplicity and simultaneity of ties within the serial researcher's life nicely captures a similar quality in the life of the research system, while also suggesting points at which systemic agendas are shaped by key individuals. Thirdly, we see how within the individual research strategy specific events like a workshop or a new project proposal become opportunities for work in a series of contexts. A workshop on emission trading instruments is also an interview location for an ESRC project, and a linkage to an OECD programme on environment and technology. With identities shifting in this fashion, EU projects can no longer be located simply in their catchy acronyms, coded project references and codified contracts.

The Life of a Project

The above approach focuses on an elite, core group of research barons. Since these individuals represent only a minority of people in the social environmental community, we introduce another layer of life beyond the European machine. Here it is the life of a project, rather than the individual narrative that reveals the plethora of linkages between programmes. The key point here is that any project is typically part of a literal and virtual chain of projects. There is a real chain, in that project X emerges from contacts made and ideas generated in a prior project; in turn, X generates a new funded project or, at least, a proposal for new funding! However, project X itself contains a multiplicity of other projects, in that different partners and their research assistants each carry their own interests and backgrounds, and inevitably differ in their interpretations of what needs to be done. This is especially apparent in large research teams that may have been hastily put together by a core group of people, thus creating 'shotgun weddings'. The following description of a fictional project helps illustrate these observations.

Sustainability, Transport and Public Attitudes (SUSTRAP)
Project funded by the European Union (EU) DGXII
Project reference: ENV4980645
May 1996–April 1998
Coordinator:
Professor K. Johansson, Institute for Environmental Politics, University of Copenhagen, Denmark
Partners:
Professor S. Brown, Management School, Manchester University, UK
Dr de Laat, Department of Technology and Society, University of Amsterdam, the Netherlands
R. Leconte, Centre for Environmental Management, France
Dr V.Cortez, Department of Economics, Universidad Autonoma de Madrid, Spain

Autumn 1995
De Laat and Brown are at a lunch meeting in connection with an EU project on sustainability and consumption. They happen to get talking about Brown's work for Manchester City Council on public attitudes to the environment. One of the partners from Aarhus chips in and mentions that Johansson, a well-known political science colleague who recently moved to Copenhagen, is working on methods for public participation. Somebody mentions that the EU is looking to expand research on the public in relation to the environment in its upcoming framework programme, the launching of which is due in a month's time. A new EU project has been born.

Some discussion follows on possible sectors to focus on. De Laat, a cultural anthropologist, is personally keen on emerging questions in genetically modified organisms. Brown, who has a background in engineering, favours energy efficiency. They leave the meeting, each promising to think some more about this.

Back home, Brown finds a letter from a French colleague, Faucheux, along with a set of recent papers on sustainable transport – transportation and construction being an area that Brown used to work on three years back. Brown invites Faucheux to become involved in the EU project idea; Faucheux, who is too busy, suggests the name of Leconte, who agrees. Brown and Leconte share a background in science and technology studies, so they are able to find common ground quickly and settle on public transport as the sector to be studied. The political scientist, Johansson, is contacted and invited to be the coordinator; she believes that, since there have been a number of experiments in public participation, it is time for something on public attitudes to participation. Personally, she hopes to link up the work with the literature on policy evaluation. Only de Laat's interests in new cultural dilemmas seem to have been squashed out, but he needs to find a new project for one of his research assistants and, anyway, he tells himself, these projects can always turn out in unexpected ways! A Spanish partner is roped in, and the proposal dashed off a day before the deadline.

May 1996

It turns out that the project gets funding. A kick-off meeting follows. Even before the partners get to the table, it is clear that Brown and Johansson are the implicit leaders of the group, although the latter has contributed little to the actual writing of the proposal. Both are professors with established reputations in their areas of the field. One of them is definitely a serial operator in social environmental research; the other is getting close to deserving the label. De Laat completes the triangle of the core, being the flexible negotiator behind the scenes, and very influential in that he wrote at least half of the proposal. Each of these three players is interested in focusing the project through somewhat different approaches. Brown favours a sociotechnical network analysis in which public attitudes are shown to be determined by the material infrastructure of transport; de Laat would like a discourse-analytic perspective 'unpacking' the meanings that the public attach to different forms of transport and to the environment; Johansson is inevitably going to push for a rapid settlement into a policy evaluation framework and criteria. Each of them has a research assistant who will be carrying out the bulk of the fieldwork. Two of these researchers have worked on related themes before and are hoping to incorporate this research into PhD theses. Leconte is a lone research consultant whose unit is entirely self-funded.

April 1997

Over a series of meetings in the past year, the project witnessed many lively debates, a few serious threats based on fundamental methodological disagreements, and took several twists and turns. As a consequence, the research has made less progress than projected in the proposal and, although still within the project description, threatens to veer off into different directions. Johansson, the coordinator, is getting concerned about producing not only the final deliverables but also clear policy recommendations. To emphasize the importance of 'policy relevance', she invites policy makers she knows from the Danish national committee of IHDP and from the Transport and the Environment Ministry to the SUSTRAP project meeting.

Other partners share her observation that a (new) convergence has to be established and welcome the interaction with 'users', but they also want to minimize extra workload. After a two-day meeting in which each of the partners carefully tries to sail through the Scylla of the project and the Charybdis of their own interests and time, a few weeks follow in which Johansson and de Laat manage to finalize a work schedule for the rest of the project.

April 1998

The project formally ends with a set of written reports and a special issue of a leading journal in the works. There is also a proposal for a book contract. Brown's assistant has sent in a PhD funding proposal to the ESRC, which essentially repackages the European work for the national market. Johansson's assistant has already been working some of the material into her thesis. De Laat has linked up with one of the members of the project advisory board and is writing a joint proposal to the EU for funding on attitudes to genetically modified organisms, among other things.

The project life described above is again fictional, but constructed from various experiences related to us in the course of our interviews with project researchers. In short, SUSTRAP germinated from another EU project and itself generated a new EU project, as well as an ESRC proposal and two PhD theses. During its life, it was already made up of several different projects for the various partners and other researchers, each of whom had different motivations for getting involved. By finding its way into a variety of other settings – presentations at workshops and conferences, smaller funding proposals for network-building or exchange workshops, input at planning or advisory committee meetings, and so on – SUSTRAP can be seen as the node in a chain of projects that connect different parts and players of the European social environmental research system. However, it is not a stable node with a fixed identity. Easily traced in EU databases through its acronym, and bridled by a contract, it sweeps between SUSTRAP project meetings and localized research activities. The localization of the research in other contexts makes the project simultaneously ENV4980645, PhD research, research on a policy evaluation framework, a study of public attitudes, a preparation for an ESRC project and a workshop where a national IHDP committee meets policy makers.

EUROPEAN DYNAMICS AND THE EU SOCIAL ENVIRONMENTAL RESEARCH PROGRAMME

Analysing the organization of the EU Human Dimensions programme in relation to other international programmes, various linkages came to the fore. The threads connecting these programmes or systems could represent individual researchers, agendas and project funds. The point is that programme machines are linked in a multiplicity of ways through the simultaneous flow of people, ideas and money. The networks they give rise to are numerous and vary in many respects, yet together they ensure the circulation of capacity, resources and ideas, and, hence, influence, from one programme – or network – to another. At the same time, the linkages cut across individual, national and international levels of activity. The hierarchical image that we tend to associate with talk of 'levels' gives way to an image of a space or landscape within which these levels coexist and interact in ways that make them interdependent. To circumvent the image of different, hierarchical levels, we coined the notion of a 'network of networks'.

But how is social environmental research constituted within this network of networks? What happens with programmes, with projects and with researchers if they are part of such a web? More specifically, what is the EU programme within such a regime and how can it fulfil its subsidiary role of subsidizing research with European added value? What, after all, is this added value, if the programme is welded into the fabric of interrelated programmes, institutes and networks? Are the 'EU programme', the 'EU projects' and the 'EU partici-pants' entangled by the myriad of linkages, or do they move through it like a spider? These questions have been dealt with in the previous sections in two ways: as a question on the conceptualization of the European dynamics of social environmental research, and as a question on the effects of the EU programme inspired by the tension between the principle of subsidiarity, on the one hand, and of unification, on the other.

Our explorations of the machinery of the EU programme, of the diaries of a serial operator and of the life of a project show that the processes by which the nodes of the networks are linked do more than just this job of linkage. Crucially, they also shape and help construct the identity of these nodes. Research evolves from work programmes and calls for proposals via a set of projects and the cumulative results of these projects. Researchers functioning as contractors for environmental knowledge within the EU programme act as programme managers within other contexts. Research projects funded by a national programme may become part of international activities. Research papers are taken from one locality to another, moving from a 'greening of industry' to a text on 'environmental technology'.

To capture the simultaneous differences and similarities between entities at different places and at different points in time, Mol and Law (1994) introduce the notion of a *fluid space*. They introduce the notion with respect to a different empirical context, the disease anaemia in its effects and related health practices in different places in time. In the fluid space it is not possible to determine identities nice and neatly, once and for all, as in the case of our EU network of networks. The fluid space is filled with mixtures of various entities: programmes, institutes, committees, researchers, and so on. In this context, what was a work programme with a set of four well-defined research areas becomes a list of projects which only partially run through these areas and often overflow their boundaries.

If this is the case, how are we to conceive of the effects of the Human Dimensions programme? Are we not throwing away the baby with the bath water (the fluid), or even drowning it in the bathtub (the fluid space), by presenting such an image of perpetual contingency? Here we would emphasize that the fluid space has its springs and fluids have their beds through which they run, although they might overflow it. The fluidity of the EU research programme should not prevent us from an understanding of specific *patterns* of activity within its regime: those that we have already explored. Fluids, after all, flow, not on account of some inexplicable natural force, but by (in our case) the practices and strategies of research managers and researchers.

The main aim of the Human Dimensions programme was to improve the basis of policies and actions in support of sustainable development in the EU. That objective conformed in all aspects to the principle of subsidiarity defined by the 'Reisenhuber criteria'. This aim would imply a development of the programme with clear boundaries, designated by the Commission's staff at DGXII as developing indicators of sustainable development; evaluating policy instruments (taxation, regulation and so on); and providing up-to-date intelligence about people's environmental values. The programme and the projects, however, did much more. Their processes for soliciting and selecting proposals established a space for social environmental researchers and projects in which they could link up with other research activities as well. As such, the programme contributed to the principle of competitiveness and social cohesion through unification.

Yet the fluidity of the programme also allowed it to interact with national and international initiatives. Perhaps these interactions were even more important for the functioning of the programme than conforming to the principles of subsidiarity and unification. Certainly, they were crucial for the SEER and Human Dimensions programme's role within the field of social environmental research. It could absorb current findings, developments and ideas within the social environmental research field; also, rather than being isolated, it could become strongly connected to the knowledge practices of the field, profiting, for example, from current processes of quality control and agenda setting.

In the next, concluding chapter, we explore the implications of this analysis for European and international research management.

6. New agendas, new dynamics: charting the development of social environmental research

INTRODUCTION

With hindsight we can appreciate that the impulse for much of the research we have documented has changed course. In 1999, the European Commission's Fifth Framework Programme, the successor programme to the one for which this research was undertaken, no longer includes a work programme explicitly labelled 'the human dimensions of environment and climate'. The small team of project officers responsible for administering this area of research has dispersed and moved on to other roles. The Fifth Framework Programme pays much more attention to sustainability, if not 'the environment', as a component of more of its Key Actions. In this, as in other ways, national and international research landscapes continue to evolve, adding new resources here, removing them from there: yet the field known as social environmental research is not about to end. The activities and agendas, not to mention the research careers we describe in this book, will undoubtedly unfold and develop in ways we cannot anticipate in any detail.

This concluding chapter represents the culmination of our analysis and provides a review of the ideas and insights we have developed along the way. Starting with national case studies and a comparison of national infrastructures of social environmental research, we moved on through successive investigations of research agendas, research careers and other forms of international funding. In the process we developed a new analytic language, not of research systems and transnational institutions, but of flows and circulations of people, resources and ideas. We did this in an attempt to better capture the dynamics of international research in the social environmental arena. In this last part of the book we explore the implications of our 'network of networks' model for researchers, for research policy makers and for the substance of social environmental research.

In Chapter 5, we outlined an approach to the analysis of European research relationships using the concepts of flow and circulation and the idea of 'boundary objects'. The aim of this was to help explain the emergence of shared preoccupations within the international research community and between research and policy. We suggested that research agendas have the important function of linking, or appearing to link, potentially divergent interests. What are the characteristics of research themes which fit the overlapping expectations of policy sponsors, on the one hand, and the research community, on the other? How do these features together shape what constitutes European social environmental research? In addressing these questions, we asked whether research agendas were inadvertently dominated by the positions and priorities of a small, but well informed and well-connected, research elite or by the pressures and demands of research management.

We also attended to questions of content. Encompassing themes such as 'ecological modernization' span and unite diverse channels of thought and debate in research and policy. We argued that coordination at the level of ideas was important, in that it provides a common point of reference for a wider community of research funders, who keep watch on each other's priorities. The first section of this concluding chapter focuses on the theoretical and practical implications of such intellectual convergence.

Elsewhere in the book we acknowledged the creative, sometimes subversive, ways in which researchers navigate between funders' research agendas and, in the process, carve out intellectual careers and research trajectories of their own making. These observations point to another way of thinking about the emergence of new agendas and remind us of the fact that research providers have their own priorities and ambitions, and their own ways of realizing those goals.

Opportunities for integrating research and policy reflect similar tensions and dynamics. Looking back over the content of research supported under the 'social environmental' banner, we detected a move away from a broad programme of enquiry which opened and addressed questions about the nature of sustainability and societal pathways towards that goal, to a much narrower research agenda organized around the development of indicators, instruments and clean technologies. This focusing of research activity reflects an increasingly explicit concern with policy relevance and with the added value, and practical utility, of work funded by the European Union. That much is clear. However, the day-to-day linkages between research and policy remain elusive. Exactly who is expected to benefit from research, and how is interaction between research and policy organized?

We suggest that anticipations and expectations of policy relevance constitute another important coordinating device. Well founded or not, ideas about the research needs of environmental policy makers have implications for the day-to-day conduct of research policy and for the detailed design of research practice. The circulation of policy preoccupations within and between countries makes a difference to the shape and character of the research agenda, as do expectations of the proper division of labour between the social and natural sciences. It is also possible to discern movements in what we might term 'research practices' on the part of institutions: for example, the involvement of research 'users' and 'beneficiaries' in research activities, and the priority now attached to the dissemination and diffusion of research results. In the second section of this chapter, we turn our attention to the relationship between concepts of policy relevance and the shaping of social environmental research.

The final section takes us back to some of the questions with which we began: how have European social environmental research agendas and networks developed and how have these been steered and shaped by national and international research and science policy? Returning to these questions in light of our ideas about the 'network of networks', and about the flow and accumulation of research priorities, research expertise and research reputations, we reconsider the notion that research funders steer and programme research activity. This prompts further thought about ways in which international research funders might intervene in a world of mutually influential and interdependent networks of researchers, research ideas and researcher–user relationships. In conclusion, this leads us to consider approaches to research policy making which take account of the interinstitutional circulation of people, resources and ideas.

SOCIAL ENVIRONMENTAL ENQUIRY: CONVERGENCE AND FRAGMENTATION

Our research supports the view that 'environmental' research is, in practice, a moveable feast. What constitutes the environment varies widely in perception as well as in practice and policy between disciplines and countries. Efforts to initiate a Europe-wide social environmental research agenda are set against this fractured and fragmented background. Like it or not, some form of convergence, and some pulling together of ideas about the limits and possibilities of environmental research, was a precondition for the shaping of a European programme. For reasons we have already outlined, themes of clean technology and ecological modernization have played an important part in this process; but need that have been the case? Other questions and issues, for instance about pathways towards sustainability, or the nature of a sustainable society, featured prominently in early work programmes but were successively edged to the margins of debate.

We can now consider three interrelated explanations for this particular form of convergence. Were agendas 'captured' by researchers and steered towards areas of existing expertise? There have been long-standing debates about the tension between academic autonomy and the risks of capture, allied to the fear that tried and tested researchers might dominate a field to the exclusion of unknown but promising 'young blood'. Such discussions generally focus on who acquires what positions within traditional research institutions; on the unintended consequences of peer review, and so on. To this we would add the further consideration of accumulated, national and transnational credibility. Does the intersection of national and international research agenda setting enhance researchers' ability to trade ideas and proposals across frontiers, so building their international reputation and thereby securing a tighter grip on the substance of social environmental research? Though it was relatively easy to identify a core group of research 'barons', this does not in itself explain either the extent to which the European social environmental research agendas have converged or why that narrowing process should have had one focus rather than another.

A second possibility is that certain ideas and, in particular, the concept of ecological modernization, exerted a kind of magnetic force on the research field. Was this an emblematic agenda which, by linking together policy and research priorities, had the power to pull researchers into the picture and sweep them off their feet? The policy appeal of concepts like clean technology and the seemingly self-evident need for social scientific analysis of related policy instruments and public perceptions is surely part of the story. But does this mean that social scientists had, or have, no opportunity to intervene or to create space for a more critical and a more challenging role? Were they simply caught up in a stream of funding and in an intellectual process which was impossible to resist?

Our work suggests that both possibilities are at play. As well as observing a form of closure, evident in the text of individual work programmes and evidently initiated by the formal agenda setters and their policy making masters, we also recognize a measure of independence on the part of research providers. Again it is important to remember that research requires researchers. However, we argue that the form of mutual influence is more subtle and more complex than is usually recognized. This is especially so when we take account of the national and international dynamics at play.

A third possibility is that the multiple networks through which research and funding are bound together have the unintended consequence of favouring the circulation of certain sorts of themes and positions. In the field of social environmental research we have identified a range of national and international research funders. Though each has its own rules, agendas and ambitions, these are developed not in isolation but through a process of fairly constant observation and mutual adjustment. This in itself fosters a measure of convergence. On the other hand, we have also learned something about researchers' strategies for dealing with such complex and demanding funding regimes. The practice of 'selling' similar research to different funding bodies, and of developing ideas sparked off by one project through a succession of other, technically unrelated, studies makes sense: especially since it is this kind of private research programming which allows researchers to retain some control over their own careers and identities.

Again we see the intersection of different strands: formal agendas are inter-related as funders seek to benefit from or add value to each other's initiatives. Meanwhile, the private agendas of researchers are pieced together, project by project, through the strategic assembly of technically separate pieces of research. Our research suggests that opportunities for convergence and creative portfolio management change as the networks of research, policy and research management coevolve. In this context, the multiplication of agencies involved in funding social environmental research seems to have the paradoxical effect of narrowing rather than broadening the research agenda.

EUROPEAN RESEARCH AND ENVIRONMENTAL POLICY: RELEVANCE AND PRACTICE

We have been looking at a specific research area, that of environmental research, and the role of social science within it. When the first call for proposals went out under the EU's SEER programme, there was no recognizable research community, and no ready-made set of priorities or established preoccupations. The environment represented a new departure for social science: interest had to be courted and cultivated, capacity had to be built and new issues carved out. What followed has been strongly influenced by interpretations of what it is the social sciences might have to offer and what contribution they can and should make in the context of natural science and policy.

Expectations of role and relevance form part of the policy and research landscape we have described. As well as setting the scene in which formal work programmes are designed, they also influence the framing of research problems and the evaluation of what follows. Our work highlights three especially important themes regarding the relationship between environmental social science and policy.

Interpretations of relevance are typically driven by second guesses about what policy makers will or will not find useful. The link between research and policy is powerfully mediated by the views and opinions of those who act as gatekeepers and intermediaries, acting on behalf of real policy makers but not making policy themselves. Judgments about policy-relevant and researchable questions, and about appropriate routes for dissemination and influence, are consequently made with reference to second-hand models and images of the way research is really used.

In this inherently uncertain context, we have learned to appreciate the importance of shared themes and concepts which help to define the contours of common ground. Such orienting ideas have a vital part to play in offering a semblance of unity and in that way facilitating the coexistence of what are ultimately contrasting perspectives. The notion that member states and the EU can find ways of linking economy with environment and that there are no lasting contradictions between these goals represents one such unifying theme. Rephrased in research terms, such a position has the positive advantage of legitimizing projects examining the beliefs and attitudes of 'green' consumers through to studies of innovation and industries based on clean technology. Both form part of the 'same' analysis of environmental improvement. In short, we argue that ecological modernization represents a model and a theoretical perspective which meshes, somewhat uncontroversially, with policy, and which also generates a spread of tractable, researchable questions.

We have seen how research agendas flow back and forth between member states, and shown how those which find favour share certain institutional characteristics. Similar points can be made about environmental policy itself. Questions of subsidiarity and added value structure the formation of environmental policy within the EU. Policy positions and preoccupations move within and between policy communities. Definitions of environment do the same. In both cases the concept of boundary objects serves us well. We can, for instance, understand how nation states see themselves in EU policy, and how policy agendas at the same time span divergent interests.

The points above concern the link between social science and policy, but what of the interface with the natural sciences? The SEER and Human Dimensions of Environmental Change programmes placed particular emphasis on interdisciplinarity, but on whose terms? Where natural science dominates, social science is typically positioned in the role of providing explanations for policies, practices and technologies not working as expected, and of analysing the behavioural factors involved. Equally, where social science dominates, internal disciplinary preoccupations limit, and often prevent, interaction with other experts and debates.

To summarize, despite their claims and ambitions, transnational research programmes on the environment inhabit an uncertain space between actual policy and research: there are few linkages or mechanisms for relating one to the other. Yet the concept of policy relevance is extremely influential. Hence we observe the impact of powerful images of what policy requires of social science – often defined with respect to natural science, and to a somewhat conservative and restrictive agenda.

What is delivered, on the other hand, does not necessarily conform to what was promised. Social researchers persist in pursuing their own interests, albeit within the dominant paradigm of ecological modernization. This is the context in which EU project officers face the daily challenge of trying to deliver policy-relevant research while having only limited control over what actually goes on. In addition, we see them caught between trying to reshape policy expectations of social science and trying to meet them at the same time.

INTERNATIONAL RESEARCH POLICY AND NETWORK MANAGEMENT

What is the meaning of research policy in a world where there are so many research funders and providers and in which there are so many cross-cutting but also overlapping motivations? Despite the time and effort invested in drafting work programmes and calls for proposals, we have to reject the notion that research directions can be so deliberately set or that research agendas can be steered, single-handed. Even a quick review of social environmental research programmes reveals an array of national preoccupations, some of which define the context within which others develop. One agenda influences another. Recognizing this point, our network of networks model emphasizes the extent to which ideas spread horizontally, as well as vertically, and flow between as well as through research systems. This model also underlines the importance of social contacts and interaction: when it comes to the dissemination and formulation of research ideas, who you know is at least as important as what you know.

However, contacts alone are not enough. It is also important to be able to put these to good use, and to build credibility and reputation, step by step. The result is an uneven landscape populated by key figures and especially important players who make a difference to the weight of argument and the directions in which research is pursued.

Our work has demonstrated the value of understanding the preoccupations and career trajectories of individual researchers as a means of understanding the place which EU-funded research has in their lives and in the lives of their institutions and research centres. As we have shown, EU funding can enhance existing reputations, and it can also mark the start of a whole new career, especially for new research assistants drawn into the field as a result of project funding. Research policy makers and research managers tend to focus on the fate of research, not of the researchers involved, yet our work suggests that personal careers and networks are at least as important when it comes to the promotion and evolution of policy-relevant research.

The form of research funding is an important consideration. The rules and conditions of research support have relevant, if indirect, implications for the sorts of networks engendered as a result. We have seen, for instance, that EU programmes provide a testing ground for ideas and create space in which research careers, teams and institutes acquire credibility and reputation. The fact that EU project teams are multinational has a really profound impact on the micro-level organization of research activity and the evolution of networks and agendas at the project level as well as the programme level. Participants are involved for their own reasons and motivations, and these have a significant influence on what work is done and how it is coordinated, organized and promoted.

More directly, and as one might expect, EU spending has undoubtedly created research capacity, especially in new areas like social environmental research. Things are happening which would not otherwise have occurred, people are drawn in ways that would not otherwise be the case, and genuinely new networks are forged and formed as a result. In reflecting on this process it is important to remember that this is a young field still populated by first-generation agenda setters who have had the opportunity to become what we term 'serial operators'. Research groups have been established and are becoming institutionalized on the back of this work, but what of the future? Will a new generation take over? If so, is this the generation of research assistants now working on social environmental projects or will some other population intervene?

Durable centres of expertise appear through careful, sometimes strategic, playing of the research game: funding is sought and found from different sources, leading to the accumulation of knowledge, and hence the right to a role in setting the agendas of the future. But survival also depends on flexibility and on being able to explore new issues and follow fashions as required.

To return to the question with which we began this section: what does it mean to be an international research policy maker in this world of overlapping networks? What is the capacity for intervention and action and what kind of research policy is it possible to develop? The notion of single-handed agenda setting is misleading, yet there are avenues of influence not only regarding research providers but also with reference to other funders. As key nodes in the network of networks we have described, international research funders have an important part to play in the competition for and the circulation of ideas, money and people. Their capacity for action and intervention lies in their ability to influence the flow of all three 'currencies' across the landscape of European social environmental research.

In making this point, we argue for a new approach to the analysis of research and funding. Scientific knowledge is typically represented as the product of individual research activity, and as something which crosses boundaries and circulates freely between countries. Some might even argue that science is inherently international in this respect. On the other hand, the worlds of science are also described in terms of the institutions in which research takes place; the national funding structures and research councils which make it possible; the efforts of governments and others to steer the course of enquiry; and, more recently, the role of international projects, networks and programmes.

In mainstream science policy literature the organizational structures of science are typically characterized in terms of a national perspective, as in comparative reviews of national research systems, or in more historical studies of relevant institutions. If the international level is involved, it is as an aggregated collection of national systems (Cozzens *et al.*, 1990), a battlefield where national interests meet, or a system in its own right but one which can be analysed in terms similar to those used to understand research practices in individual countries.

Such approaches avoid the rather obvious point that international research activity involves people who also, at the same time, have national identities and careers. In practice, all three layers – the individual, the national and the international – interact. In practice, too, this interaction of individual strategies and national regimes generates further tensions and possibilities on the international plane: tensions which we need to understand if we are to make sense of the conditions and circumstances of transnational or, in our case, European social environmental research.

One goal of this book has been to develop ways of understanding the dynamics of international social science which take due account of this multiplication and intersection of national and transnational practice. Another has been to analyse the shape and character of European social science research and the values and commitments it embodies. National and international research programmes generally aim to produce knowledge and insights of practical value for policy making. Systems of research management are designed with this end in mind, and with the aim of directing scientific energies and imaginations towards this goal. The benefits of academic freedom and the risks of scientific capture go hand in hand and research systems exemplify different responses to this enduring dilemma (Braun, 1998; Guston, 1996; Rip, 1995; van der Meulen, 1998). However carefully designed, these arrangements assume a bounded world in which a clearly defined research community interacts with an equally well-specified population of research funders and users. In the context of European social environmental research, this is simply not the case.

National and international research funders confront what seems to be an increasingly elusive research community. Research providers are now skilled in crossing borders and catering for more than one sponsor at the same time. Though research sponsors have specific policy agendas, research providers have ambitions of their own. As we have seen, research groups selectively construct their own long-term identities by picking and choosing projects which meet their needs as well as the needs of the funding agency involved. Though funders control the purse strings, what happens also depends on the interests and aspirations of researchers bent on assembling coherent research portfolios of their own making.

These insights have prompted us to ask new questions about the substance of social environmental research and about the limits and possibilities of international research programme management. Having switched attention away from the analysis of national or even international research systems, and focused it instead on the coordinating functions of agendas and networks, we have to acknowledge the contingent character of 'social environmental research'. Rather than seeing the field developing in response to known research needs or emerging around a menu of self-evidently important problems, we have recognized that there are no neat beginnings and endings. This is also true of the work on which this book is based. As in the research worlds we have been describing, our own project continues to live on, albeit in modified and characteristically hybrid ways: Barend and Liana are partners in another EU project; Sujatha and Elizabeth continue to work together; Pablo has spent some time at the University of Twente and developed contacts there; Heide and Barend are now colleagues; Michael has moved to a new department which houses MEDALUS, the largest EU grant on the physical environment. New networks are being formed, and new agendas continue to unfold.

References

Bailey, F.G. (1969), *Stratagems and Spoils: A Social Anthropology of Politics*, Oxford: Blackwell.

Barnes, B. and D.O. Edge (eds) (1982), *Science in Context: Readings in the Sociology of Science*, Milton Keynes: Open University Press.

Beck, U. (1995), *Ecological Politics in an Age of Risk*, Cambridge: Polity Press.

Benton, T. (1994), 'Biology and Social Theory in the Environmental Debate', in M.R. Redclift and T. Benton (eds), *Social Theory and the Global Environment*, London: Routledge.

Braun, D. (1998), 'The role of funding agencies in the cognitive development of science', *Research Policy*, 27 (8), 807–21.

Cozzens, S.E., P. Healey, A. Rip and J. Ziman (eds) (1990), *The Research System in Transition*, Boston: Kluwer.

Deblonde, M.K. (1996), 'Environmental Economic Scientists and Politics', *Innovation: The European Journal of Social Sciences*, 9 (4),449–58.

DiMaggio, P. and W. Powell (eds) (1991), *The New Institutionalism in Organizational Analysis*, Chicago: University of Chicago Press.

Eder, K. (1996), 'The Institutionalisation of Environmentalism: Ecological Discourse and the Second Transformation of the Public Sphere', in S. Lash, B. Szerszynski and B. Wynne (eds), *Risk, Environment and Modernity; Towards a New Ecology*, London: Sage.

European Commission (1993), *White Paper from the European Commission on Growth, Competitiveness and Employment*, Brussels: Commission of the European Communities.

European Commission (1996), *Environment and Climate 1994–1998, Work Programme and Information Package*, Brussels: Commission of the European Communities.

European Commission (1998a), *Commission Opinion on Accession: Synthesis Report*, Brussels: Commission of the European Communities.

European Commission (1998b), *Preserving the Ecosystem: Energy, Environment and Sustainable Development, Annex II,* Brussels: Commission of the European Communities.

European Commission (1998c), *Research on the Socio-economic Aspects of Environmental Change: Summary results (1992–1996)*, Luxembourg: Office for Official Publications of the European Communities, EUR 18453.

Fousekis, P. and J.N. Lekakis (1997), 'Greece's Institutional Response to Sustainable Development', *Environmental Politics*, 6 (1),131–52.

Gibbons, M., C. Limoges, H. Nowotny, S. Schwartzman, P. Scott and M. Trow (1994), *The New Production of Knowledge*, London: Sage.

The Globe (1997), *Special Issue on Global Environmental Networks, The Globe*, 38, August.

Golub, J. (ed.) (1998), *Global Competition and EU Environmental Policy*, London: Routledge.

Gouldson, A. and J. Murphy (1996), 'Ecological Modernization and the European Union', *Geoforum*, 27 (1), 11–21.

Guston, D.H. (1996), 'Principal–agent theory and the structure of science policy', *Science and Public Policy*, 23 (4), 229–40.

Guzzetti, L. (1995), *A Brief History of European Union Research Policy*, Brussels: Commission of the European Communities.

Haas, P.M. (1989), 'Do regimes matter? Epistemic communities and Mediterranean pollution control', *International Organisation*, 43, 377–403.

Haas, P.M. (1992), 'Epistemic Communities and International Policy Coordination: Introduction', *International Organization*, 46 (1), 1–35.

Hagstrom, W.O. (1965), *The Scientific Community*, New York: Basic Books.

Hajer, M.A. (1997), *The Politics of Environmental Discourse: Ecological Modernization and the Policy Process*, Oxford: Clarendon Press.

Hannigan, J. (1995), *Environmental Sociology: a Social Constructionist Perspective*, London: Routledge.

Huber, J. (1982), *Die verlorene Unschuld der Okologie*, Frankfurt am Main: Fisher.

Huber, J. (1985), 'Ecologische modernisering', in E. van den Abbeele (ed.), *Ontmanteling van de groei*, Nijmegen: Markant.

Jamison, A. (1996), 'The Shaping of the Global Environmental Agenda: The Role of Non-Governmental Organisations', in S. Lash B. Szerszynski and B. Wynne (eds), *Risk, Environment and Modernity: Towards a New Ecology*, London: Sage.

Janicke, M. (1988), 'Okologische Modernisierungen' in U.E. Simonis (ed.), *Preventive Umweltpolitik*, Frankfurt am Main: Campus Verlag.

Jasanoff, S. and B. Wynne (1998), 'Science and decisionmaking', in S. Rayner and E.I. Malone (eds), *Human Choices and Climate Change, Vol 1: The Societal Framework*, Colombus, Ohio: Battelle Press.

Krasner, S.D. (ed.), (1983), *International Regimes*, Ithaca: Cornell University Press.

Kwa, C. (1993), 'Modelling technologies of control', *Science as Culture*, 4 (2), 363–91.

Latour, B. and S. Woolgar (1979), *Laboratory Life*, London: Sage Publications.

Liberatore, A. (1994), 'Facing global warming: The interactions between science and policy-making in the European community', in M.R. Redclift and T. Benton (eds), *Social Theory and the Global Environment*, London: Routledge.

Liefferink, J.D., P.D. Lowe and A.P.J. Mol (eds) (1995), *European Integration and Environmental Policy*, Chichester: John Wiley.

Lonergan, S., M. Brklacich, C. Cocklin, N.P. Gleditsch, E. Gutierrez-Espeleta, F. Langeweg, R. Matthew, S. Narain and M. Soroos (1999), *Global Environmental Change and Human Security: Science Plan*, Bonn: International Human Dimensions Programme (IHDP), IHDP report no. 11.

Lowe, P. and S. Ward (eds) (1998), *British Environmental Policy and Europe*, London: Routledge.

Luhmann, T. (1989), *Ecological Communication*, Chicago: University of Chicago Press.

Lundvall, B.A. (ed.), (1992), *National Systems of Innovation*, New York: St Martin's Press.

Merton, R. (1973), *The Sociology of Science*, Chicago: University of Chicago Press.

Mol, A. and J. Law (1994), 'Regions, Networks and Fluids: Anaemia and Social Topology', *Social Studies of Science*, 24, 641–71.

Mulberg, J. (1996), 'Modernity and Environmental Economics: A Sociological Critique', *Innovation: The European Journal of Social Sciences*, 9 (4), 435–48.

Nelson, R.R. (ed.) (1993), *National Innovation Systems: A Comparative Analysis*, Oxford: Oxford University Press.

Newby, H. (1991), 'One world, two cultures: sociology and the environment', *British Sociological Association Bulletin: Network*, 50 (May),1–8.

OECD (1991), *Choosing Priorities in Science and Technology*, Paris: OECD Publications.

OECD (1992), *Government Options to Promote Cleaner Production and Products in the Nineties*, Paris: OECD/GD(92)127.

Pearce, D., A. Markandaya and E. Barbier (1989), *Blueprint for a Green Economy*, London: Earthscan.

Price, M.F. (1990), 'Humankind in the biosphere', *Global Environmental Change*, December, 3–13.

Rayner, S. and E.I. Malone (eds) (1998), *Human Choices and Climate Change* (4 vols), Colombus, Ohio: Battelle Press.

Redclift, M. (1987), *Sustainable Development: exploring the contradictions*, London: Routledge.

Redclift, M. and T. Benton (eds) (1994), *Social Theory and the Global Environment*, London: Routledge.

Redclift, M. and C.Sage (eds) (1994), *Strategies for Sustainable Development: local agendas for the Southern Hemisphere*, Chichester: John Wiley and Sons.

Redclift, M. and G.Woodgate (eds) (1998) *The International Handbook of Environmental Sociology*, Cheltenham: Edward Elgar.

Rip, A. (1995), 'The post-modern research system', *Nature*, September, 28–9.

Rip, A. (1999), 'Aggregation machines: a political science of science approach to the future of the peer review system', in W.N. Dunn, M. Hisschemoller, R. Hoppe and J.R. Ravetz (eds), *Knowledge, Power and Participation in Risk Policymaking*, Policy Studies Annual Review, forthcoming.

RMNO (1994), *Inventory of International Networks in the Field of the Human Dimensions of Global Environmental Change: the Involvement of the Netherlands Research Community*, Rijswijk: RMNO, Publication no. 103.

RMNO (1996), *Research Activities on Nature and Environment: Overview of national and international programmes and organisations*, Rijswijk: RMNO, Publication no. 114.

Schot, J., E. Brand and K. Fischer (1997), *The Greening of Industry for a Sustainable Future, Building an International Research Agenda*, Rijswijk: GIN and RMNO, report no. 123.

Shove, E. (2000), 'Reputations, Reciprocities and Social Science Research', in M. Jacob and T. Hellstrom (eds), The Future of Knowledge Production in the Academy, Open University Press.

Simonis, U.E. (1989), 'Ecological modernisation of industrial society: three strategic elements', *International Social Science Journal*, 121, 347–61.

Spaargaren, G. (1997), 'The Ecological Modernization of production and consumption', PhD thesis, University of Wageningen, The Netherlands.

Spaargaren, G. and A. Mol (1992), 'Sociology, environment and modernity', *Society and Natural Resources*, 5 (4), 323–44.

Star, S.L. and J. Griesemer (1989), 'Institutional ecology, "translations" and boundary objects: amateurs and professionals in Berkeley's Museum of Vertebrate Zoology, 1907–1939', *Social Studies of Science*, 19, 387–420.

Tronner, R. and M. Penker (1999), 'Socio-Ecological Assessment as a Planning Tool for a Sustainable Development of Environmental and Agricultural Legislation', *Innovation: the European Journal of Social Sciences*, 12, forthcoming.

Turner, B.L., D.L. Skole, S. Sanderson, G. Fischer, L. Fresco and R. Leemans (eds) (1995), *Land Use and Land Cover Change. Science/ Research Plan*, Bonn: International Human Dimensions Programme; Brussels: European Commission's Environment and Climate Programme.

van der Meulen, B. (1998), 'Science policy as principal–agent games', *Research Policy*, 27 (4), 397–414.

van der Meulen, B. and A. Rip (1998), 'Mediation in the Dutch Science System', *Research Policy*, 27 (8), 757–69.

Vellinga, P. (1999), *Industrial Transformation Draft Science Plan*, Bonn: International Human Dimensions Programme (IHDP).

Vinck, D., Kahane, B., Laredo, P. and Meyer, J.B. (1993), 'A Network Approach to Studying Research Programmes: Mobilizing and Coordinating Public Responses to HIV/AIDS'. *Technology Analysis & Strategic Management*, 5 (1), 39–54.

Wagner, P., C.H. Weiss, B. Wittrock and H. Wollmann (eds) (1991), *Social Sciences and Modern States: national experiences and theoretical crossroads*, Cambridge: Cambridge University Press.

Weale, A. (1992), *The New Politics of Pollution*, Manchester: Manchester University Press.

Wittrock, B. and A. Elzinga (ed.) (1985), *The University Research System: the public policies of the home of scientists*, Stockholm: Almqvist & Wiksell.

World Commission on Environment and Development (1987), *Our Common Future*, Oxford: Clarendon Press.

Young, O. (1989), *International Cooperation: building regimes for natural resources and the environment*, Ithaca: Cornell University Press.

Young, O.R. (1999), *Science Plan: The project on the Institutional Dimensions of Global Environmental Change*, Bonn: International Human Dimensions Programme.

Index

Academy of Finland 31, 41
acid rain 27, 34, 86
    comparative responses to 78, 80
actor-network theory 71
Adams, D. 2
added value, from EU-funded research
        61–2, 94, 116, 119, 123
administrative skills 59
advisory committees 9, 108
Agenda 21 (Earth Seminar 7, 1992) 85
agriculture, sustainable production
        methods in 85
air pollution 32, 42, 90
    see also acid rain
Amsterdam Free University 102
Andringa, J. 2
Angel, D. 102
'applied' research, definitions of 23, 26
Arctic region 86
Austria
    accession to EU (1995) 27
    competition for research funding in
        40, 41
    ecological modernization and
        environmental policy in 80–81,
        82
    ecological modernization and social
        environmental research in 87
    interaction between research and
        policy in 40, 41
    Ministry of Environment (est. 1972)
        80
    National Environmental Plan (1990)
        27, 80
    national programme development in
        39, 41, 49
    research capacity in 36–8, 41
    researchers' identification with social
        environmental research
        community 49
    serial operators in 64

social environmental research
        priorities in 18, 43
social environmental research system
        in 13, 26–8, 41
Austrian Institute for Sustainability
        (OIN) 27–8, 49

Bailey, F.G. 24
Bangkok, Asian network node in 102
Barnes, B. 46
barriers to European involvement *see*
        incentives and barriers to European
        involvement
'basic' research, definitions of 23, 26
Beck, U. 6
Benton, T. 6, 96
best available technology 76
biodiversity losses 34, 100
Bonn, IHDP secretariat in 99, 106
boundary objects 16, 71, 88, 107,
        118–19, 123
    ecological modernization as 3, 18,
        71–2, 87–9, 91, 119
Braun, D. 126
Brundtland Report 5, 31
Brussels, programme managers in 8, 95,
        98, 107
bureaucratic requirements, disincentive
        effects of 51
Business Strategy and the Environment
        101
business transformation 84
'butterfly-catcher syndrome' 103

Cadenas, A. 2
calls for proposals 14, 19, 83–4, 108,
        109, 116, 122
capitalism, ecological modernization
        supporting 89–90
capture of research agendas 120–21,
        126

influence on agendas 17–18, 37, 48,
  65, 69–70, 112
participation patterns of 63–5
serial research groups 37–8, 45
short-term contracts 103
shotgun partners 57, 59, 113
Shove, E. 1, 2, 46, 47, 127
Simonis, U.E. 73
Single European Act (1987) 93
social coupling 90
social environmental research community, identification with 48–9, 51
social partnership model 80
social science, environmental 5–7
Socio-Economic Environmental
  Research (SEER) programme *see*
  SEER programme
sociology of science 46, 54, 71
Spaargaren, G. 73
Spain
  accession to EC (1986) 30
  Agrarian Plan 30
  competition for research funding in
    40, 41, 50, 51, 52
  ecological modernization and environ-
    mental policy in 81–2
  Energy Plan 30
  EU-funded environmental research in
    29
  Institute of Energy Studies 30
  interaction between research and
    policy in 41
  national programme development in
    41, 48–9, 107
  research capacity in 36–7, 41
  researchers' identification with social
    environmental research
    community 49, 51
  reward systems in 51
  serial operators in 64–5
  social environmental research
    priorities in 18, 30, 41, 42–3
  social environmental research system
    in 13, 29–30
  vocational commitment in 52, 54
Star, S.L. 3, 71, 88, 107
START *see* System for Analysis,
  Research and Training (START)
structural funds, EU 28–9
structural transformation 24, 25, 36
subsidiarity principle 94, 117, 123

Sussex, University of 38
SUSTAIN 27, 41, 49
sustainability 5, 6, 8, 72, 120
  cities and 86–7
  comparative information on 61
  ecological modernization and 75–7,
    81, 82, 84, 85, 87, 88, 105
  fictional project on sustainable
    transport 113–15
  Fifth Framework Programme and 118
  Human Dimensions Programme and
    117
  indicators of 11, 87, 109, 117, 119
  meaning of 82
  national research programmes and
    27–8, 30, 31, 34, 39, 41, 78,
    81–2, 87
  regional dimension of 27–8, 81–2, 87
  stakeholder participation and 86
Sustainability, Transport and Public
  Attitudes (SUSTRAP) (fictional
  project) 113–15
'switch-over' 73
System for Analysis, Research and
  Training (START) 99

Tackling Environmental Resource
  Management (TERM) programme
  16, 96, 102–3
  funding for 104, 106
  linkages with other programmes 94–5,
    103, 105, 112
  objectives of 102–3
  role of individual researchers in 104
  serial operators involved in 64, 110, 112
  themes of 103
  work programme of 105
team members, selection of 58–60, 108–9
technology, environmental *see* environmental technology
technology transfer 87, 93
tendering process 9, 108–10
TERM *see* Tackling Environmental
  Resource Management (TERM)
  programme
terminology, inconsistencies in 23, 82
Thatcher, Margaret 33
Third Framework Programme (1990–94)
  97
Tilburg, University of 38
timescales, of European projects 11, 56